FOUNDATION FOR SUCCESS

PREVAILING TRAVAILING INTERCESSORY PRAYER

APOSTLE CALVIN MARTIN

CO-AUTHORED BY
PROPHETESS DEBBIE JERIDO

This book was transcribed from a Four-Tape Prayer Series preached and taught by Apostle Calvin Martin. The tapes were transcribed by Debbie Jerido. All material contain was taught by Calvin Martin. The Reflection and Study section and also the Epilogue were written by co-author.

FOUNDATION FOR SUCCESS
Prevailing, Travailing, Intercessory Prayer
By Apostle Calvin Martin
Co-authored by Debbie Jerido

Copyright © 2008
International Standard Book Number:
0-9787585-2-8

Published by
Foundation for Living Water
Lithonia, GA 30038

Illustrated Praying hands drawn by
Thomas P. Port Huron, Michigan.

PRINTED IN THE UNITED STATES OF AMERICA

ACKNOWLEDGEMENTS

I give thanks to my Lord and Savior, Jesus Christ, the Author and the Finisher of my faith. He is also the Chief Intercessor as an Advocate to the Father on behalf of the church. I'm thankful to the late Apostle Calvin Martin who without his sacrificial life to be a servant of the Lord this prayer series would not be possible. I'm thankful to all of those who contributed to the production of this series in honor of a great and powerful War Time General of God.

I thank Evangelist Mary in Fort Lauderdale for being a soul winner. I thank Pastor and First Lady Bullard at Trinity Christian Fellowship for being willing obedient servants of the Lord. Apostle Martin taught me that Prevailing Prayer Don't Talk Defeat! Thank you Apostle for teaching me that you can't find a great man or woman of God unless they spend time with God in prayer. Thank you for the Apostolic Prophetic Mantle of Prayer. I thank God for resuscitating the prayer mantle in 2005 and for launching the prophetic call to a new level. Special thanks to my intensive care mentor, Apostle Eddie L. Long. Thanks to Evangelist Jenkins of Awesome Power of Prayer, a powerful praying women of God. Thanks to all of my mentors, friends and family. Special thanks to Minister Temple whose beloved son preached and taught this dynamic series on prayer. This book so captures his spirit that she said: 'You can hear him when you read this book.'

INTERCESSION MINISTRIES INC.

In reading Foundation for Success: Prevailing, Travailing, Intercessory Prayer you can hear the spirit of Apostle Calvin Martin coming through the pages. It is not hard to paint a picture in your mind of this great man of God who was clearly moved by the Holy Spirit to labor in the vineyard as an anointed Intercessor of the day and time in which he ministered. Apostle Martin truly flowed out of a gift that not many would dare to yield to. Breaking up the fallow ground, he paved the way for you and I God's Intercessors.

This material could be presented as is, a Tribute to the late Apostle Calvin Martin. I'm sure it will be an added inspiration to those in the Florida and the surrounding areas who had the opportunity to experience this remarkable teaching ministry. It would be of greater value if the biography of this man of God were added.

In addition, I pray that the transcriber desires to use this sequel of teachings as a vehicle of instruction moving forward to benefit an audience today. I look forward to seeing a duplicate of Foundation for Success: Prevailing, Travailing, Intercessory Prayer the main subject matter (prayer) as a manual for educational purposes with a study guide added.

Prophetess Eura A. Russell-Robinson,
Apostolic Prophetic Intercessor & Director
Intercession Ministries, Inc.

TABLE OF CONTENTS

PREVAILING, TRAVAILING INTERCESSORY PRAYER

Calvin Martin Ministries
School of Ministry Prayer Series
By Calvin Martin

Theme: Men ought always to pray and not faint (Luke 18:1)

This book teaches the reader that Prayer is a main essential ingredient to spiritual growth and maturity in Christ. Prayer can not be neglected and has to be cultivated as every other aspect of the church. For prayer is the foundation for success and spiritual stability in Christ. Composed and compiled from a four-tape series titled Prevailing, Travailing, and Intercessory Prayer.

Calvin Martin was indeed a powerful man of prayer. In 1988, he taught this prayer series at Trinity Christian Fellowship in Miami, Florida in an area by Cutler Ridge known as Goulds. That was twenty years ago when Trinity was a small storefront or warehouse-front church. A revival was being conducted by Apostle Martin under the tutelage of Reverend Joshua Bullard. This revival went on for weeks where God wrought signs, wonders and miracles. Testimonies would come forth witnessing to the power packed revival that had taken place. Lives would be forever changed and forever altered as a result of a man who was willing to die to self, take up his cross and follow Jesus. I hope and pray that 'you' the reader is encouraged and blessed as you take a walk on this prayer journey:

PREVAILING PRAYER

PART I

GODS LOOKING FOR FAITH

"But you say Brother Martin you don't know how it is. No, you don't know how the word is. The word is the truth! The word works! You just got to know how to work the word! You work the word by being obedient to it—and by walking in faith!"

1.1

In this lesson we are going to discuss Prevailing Prayer. The key scripture will come from Luke's Gospel chapter 18:1. Say out loud "Prevailing Prayer." "I am going to prevail in prayer so that I know that by faith I decree that I have power with God and with men!" 'And he spake a parable unto them to this end' Take note the thing that Jesus said had an end to it. When he spake, he spoke: 'that men (I'll say women too) ought always to pray and not faint.' If you pray, you won't be so easy to get upset. If you find yourself in prayer you won't easily get angry and mad. You won't be so easy to fuss, bicker, gripe and complain when you spend time in prayer! I've past up some marvelous opportunities to get mad and say things to people when I knew my flesh wanted to respond. I wouldn't say anything. I just prayed and let the incident go.

But some of you say, "I am going to give that person a piece of my mind." Who wants a piece of that old filthy thing? You want to give some one a piece of your mind and you don't even have it. The little piece you got already messed up and screwed up. You better keep the little piece you got and put it in the garbage can. Let God sanctify it. God can change your mind! I was like that. I used to say, I'm gone give them a piece of my mind. God said the bit you got all ready messed up. You need to get the mind of Christ. I'm talking about myself too. Let's thank God for the mind of Christ.

He said 'men ought always' to argue, to fuss, to gripe, to grumble, to complain? No. He said 'men ought always to pray.' So why do we fuss? Why do we gripe? Why do we complain? Can you go one-day without fussing? Can you go one-day without always nagging and running your mouth against somebody? Can you go one-day without that?

I'm learning something. I've made a lot of mistakes in my life but I'm learning to correct a lot of things. You must learn from your mistakes. You won't get so old. You won't be so aging. You won't be having heart attacks and suffering from mental stress and mental inertia if you stop all that fussing, griping and complaining. Learn to love, bless God! If you feel like your heart is weighty, you go get on your face and spill it out to God until God gets through with you. When God gets through spanking your spiritual britches you will be alright. God will hang you by your pants! Folks want to fuss! Gripe! Complain and argue! (He did this! She did that! They did this and that!) Speak in tongues bless God, when you get mad and get upset. Begin to talk to

God instead of griping, fussing, complaining, mumbling and grumbling just like the children of Israel. They mumbled and grumbled and they were destroyed! (cf. 1 Cor. 10) You got people that fuss all the time. They gripe, fuss, argue and complain all the time. If your husbands' not saved, keep your mouth shut! Leave that man alone! God will save him if you shut up and pray! I was a devil myself on the way to hell but God saved me! God can save your man if you pray! There is no problem to big that God can't solve it. There is no mountain to tall that God can't move it! There is no sorrow to deep that he can't soothe it. There's no storm to dark that God can't calm it!

I want you to know that God want us to stop that griping, that grumbling, that complaining and that bickering. God wants you to be kind, tender hearted and compassionate. You'll find out that you will get answers to your prayers when you stop all that bickering, fussing, griping, and complaining and start praying. God will start moving on your behalf. When you pray, things will happen! But you say Brother Martin you don't know how it is. No, you don't know how the word is. The word is the truth! The word works! You just got to know how to work the word! You work the word by being obedient to it—walking in faith. Listen to what God says in Luke's gospel 18:1: 'and he spake a parable unto them to this end that men ought always to pray and not faint.'

The Lord is saying to us in the book of Galatians. Don't be weary in well doing. You shall reap if you faint not. Don't give up! I don't care how long it may seem like it is taking. God's going to come through for you. God's going to meet that need. God's going to make the devil out of a liar. God's going to give you the victory. You are a winner! You are an over-comer! You can make it! You can overcome! You don't have to take down! You don't have to give up. God's on your side! (cf. Gal. 6:9) The Bible says that if God be for us, who can be against us? (Rom. 8:31) He's more than your enemies against you! He's standing with you! God's holding your hand. You're going to make it! Oh yes you are! You got the word on the inside of you. All you got to do is let the word come alive in you! God is able to back up his word with power! God will part that Red Sea! God will bring you out of that Lion's Den! He'll bring you out of the Fiery Furnace! God is your deliverer! He's standing right by your side! He's ready to give you a miracle!

I can see Jesus going to a blind man. The blind man heard about Jesus. And he said, thou son of David have mercy on us. Jesus said what will thou have me to do for thee? Lord! Lord! That we might receive our sight! Jesus said bring the man here. They brought the man to Jesus. Jesus said believe ye that I am able to do this? Let me tell you before you want God to do anything you got to believe that he can do it. (cf. Mark 10:46-52)

I can also hear Shadrach, Meshach and Abednego say we're not going to bow because we're not going to burn. Our God is able! (cf. Daniel 3) I not only know that he is able. I know he is willing and I know he can! He said all things are possible to them that believe. (Mark 9:23) But if God can get you to believe, you can receive. If God can get you to believe the word of God, he can perform a miracle for you. But you got to believe the word. You got to stand in faith!

12

'For we walk by faith and not by sight' (2ⁿᵈ Cor. 5:7) The word of God says that Jesus Christ is the Author and the Finisher of our faith. 'Not looking unto man, not looking unto a woman but looking unto Jesus the author and the finisher of our faith.' (Heb. 12:2) God's going to bring you out with a mighty hand! Like he did Israel! But many of them didn't make it. The word didn't profit them. Why? They didn't mix it with faith! Anything you want from God, you got to believe the word of God and stand in faith and believe the word. That's why I'm teaching faith to you.

If you give people the word, you don't always have to lay hands on them. Give them the word! Don't give them a bunch of foolishness. Give them the word of God. I want to see the church blessed and that's why we are on our face before God. That's why we're in our secret prayer closet. We go to the church every-day and we pray for this meeting. I got people lifting this meeting up in prayer! Lifting up the pastor! Lifting this work up! The devil wants us to give up, take down, quit and walk out and say look at how everything is going.

But we're not grasshoppers in our own sight! We've got the Lord on our side. We're of a different spirit devil! We are of the spirit of Faith! We are like Joshua and Caleb. We are well able to overcome. God's looking for faith! God's looking for people to take him at his word. You must believe that God is able, not only able, but willing and know he can. Stop running around here talking about I know my God is able. You got to know that your God is willing. You got to know what God will do. Put God to the test. Put him to the test with his word. God said remind me. (cf. Isaiah 43:26)

13

THE DEFEAT OF AN ENEMY

Prevailing prayer is that kind of prayer that overcomes and gets the victory. The word prevail comes from a Greek word **Nikao**. Nikao means to overcome. From the Layman's English Greek Concordance, it means to conquer, to overcome or to get the victory. The word **victory** defined is the defeat of an enemy. Victory is the defeat of an enemy in battle. We have an enemy. We are engaged in a conflict. We are engaged in warfare! Not with flesh and blood but against principalities, and powers in the heavenlies. The King James Version says 'wicked spirits in high places'. (cf. Ephesians 6)

Webster's dictionary defines victory as the defeat of an enemy in battle or an antagonist in a contest: The superiority gained in any contest. We are battling wicked spirits in the heavenlies. We are not fighting a war of flesh and blood. The only way we can pull down strongholds and defeat that enemy is through the power of prevailing, travailing and intercessory prayer!

Travail it's like you labor. It's the depths and desire of prayer where you die. You take on the spirit. For example, we were in intercessory prayer one day and Brother Blacks took on the spirit of a little child by the name of Joshua. He took on that spirit in travail. I watched him take on that spirit at the church one-day when we were in intercessory prayer. I heard that spirit speak through him and say, "No, I won't let him go! I won't let Joshua go. I won't let him go. I'm going to take him out!"

We began to bind that spirit as Brother Blacks took it on. He got a hold to him in the realm of the spirit through travail and intercessory

14

GOD'S LOOKING FOR FAITH

prayer. Together! Locked in! Caught a hold of him! Took him on and defeated him! We got a report from Sister Steele that little Joshua—that little baby couldn't rest—that little baby couldn't sleep. That baby was struggling for his life. Sister Steele became weak, when she got the microphone, after Brother Blacks was praying. That weak spirit from that child had got on her and she rebuked it! We got the report that little Joshua is doing fine. He's doing alright. Why, because somebody travailed and interceded in prayer. Thank God for men and women of God that know the power of travail.

I want you to spend time in prayer. Prayer is beautiful! It's wonderful! Prayer is my language now. It's alright! It's sweet when you can commune with God. You will find yourselves having fewer problems. You will be less argumentative and not get into a hold bunch of strife and contention. You will begin to walk in the God kind of love. God will begin to manifest in our midst in church.

I also seen a young-man come to the altar and give his life to Christ as a result of intercessory prayer. Nobody laid hands on him. Nobody cast any spirits out of him—the spirits just cast out of him. They came out of him! Nobody touched him. Nobody said anything to him. The power of God got on him. Conviction came upon that young man and he came running to the altar crying: Ugh!!! Ugh!!! I want to give my life to Jesus! I want to give my life to Jesus!

I got excited! I like to see that type of thing. That brother began to punch all up in the air. Brother Kimble said you better watch it. I said you don't have to tell me to watch it. Big as that guy was, if he would've hit me, I would have bootlegged that big guy. I would have gone up under him. I'm a little guy but I think I could have bootlegged him! But thank God for the power of prayer.

I'm teaching you about Prevailing, Travailing and Intercessory Prayer because of what it will do and what effect it has upon us. It has an effect upon your inward man and also your outward man. Where the word of God tells us in the book of Romans, Paul said 'our outward man decayeth but our inward man is renewed day by day.' My outward man is decaying. He's feeling the affect of that prayer. He doesn't want to pray. He doesn't want to die but he's gone die. I'm not going to be body-ruled! I'm not going to be led by my flesh. I'm going to be led by the spirit of God. (cf. 2nd Cor. 4:16)

Prevailing prayer is that kind of prayer that overcomes and conquers and gets the victory. Prevailing prayer is that prayer that is effective and produces a lifeline of power with God. Prevailing prayer causes one to win, to overcome, to get the victory. I'm going to show you in Genesis how Jacob got power with God. His name was changed from Jacob which means supplanter to Israel which means one who struggles with God. Jacob struggled with God. He was wrestling.

When Brother Blacks got a hold to that spirit in the child, he was wrestling that spirit. Wrestling denotes strenuous effort. It's a fight! A conflict is going on! Somebody's going to win! But if you give in and give up, you're not going to win. Jacob didn't give in and he didn't give up. He said, I will not let you go except thy bless me.

Sometimes when we get a hold of something in the spirit realm and we know that it's not of God and we're standing in the gap, don't let it go. Hold on to it! You can bring it out of there. You can show that

16

thing that you're more than a conqueror. Christ in you, the hope of glory! The power of God! The resurrection of God! The very life of God!

The Bible says and Jacob was left alone; and there wrestled (struggled) a man with him until the breaking of the day. (Gen 32:24) All of this came about to the breaking of day. The day hadn't kind of really come in there. It's a whole lot of things go on and happen in the breaking of the day. You get up and meet with God about four o'clock or five a.m. in the morning. God will meet you there. If you say, 'God I will meet you at five a.m. in the morning'. He'll be there waiting. Some people sing those songs: *Lord I've been waiting on you.* God said I've been waiting on you too. People sing *I'm waiting, I'm waiting.* God said I'm waiting, I'm waiting too. I've been waiting for two-thousand years. Where have you been?

'And when he saw that he prevailed not (this man, this angel— he cheated) he touched the hollow of his thigh and the hollow of Jacob's thigh was out of joint'. Look at the word prevail. The scripture said when he saw that he prevailed not. The word prevail means to conquer; to overcome, to get the victory. (cf. Genesis 32:25)

THE HORNS OF THE ALTAR

Praying mothers in Christendom would say, don't you get up off of your knees until you pray through! We used that expression *pray through* or until you get the victory. Don't leave that place of prayer until you know you've got an answer from God. That's what it means to prevail. You hold on. You hang onto the horns of the altar until you know in your spirit that you have victory. The devil is fighting a losing battle! The Bible says in 1st Timothy 6:12, we are supposed to fight the good fight of faith. The word of God never told us to fight the devil. Do you know why the fight is good? Because God told me, He said, son, tell my people that faith wins the fight. 'Faith is the victory in everything.' (1st John 5:4)

1st John 5:4 says 'for whatsoever is born of God' How many of you are born of God? If you've been born of God you have overcome the world. There is the word victory. The word victory means to overcome. Faith is the victory. Victory means to overcome and to win. Faith is the victory in everything. 'For whatsoever is born of God overcometh the world. This is the victory that helpeth us to overcome the world even our faith.' So faith is the victory to help you to overcome the world.

You have world overcoming faith! But you say Brother Martin, I've sinned. I've made a mistake. I messed it up. So, you have an advocate with the Father. He is the propitiation for your sins. He is standing before God the Father pleading your case and your cause. The Bible say in the amplified version 1st John 1:19 'if we confess our sins, he is faithful. He is loyal. He is trustworthy. He is true to his word. He is faithful and just.' What do you mean just? He is just to forgive your sins—to pardon your iniquity. He is declared righteous!

FAITH IS A STRENGTH!

We emphasize here that prevailing prayer is that kind of prayer that's effective and produces a lifeline of power with God. Prevailing prayer never fails to see defeat. Now I was in prayer prevailing and God said to me, 'son prevailing prayer never fails to see defeat. Prevailing prayer don't talk defeat! It only thinks victory! It thinks the opposite of what defeat is or says.'

You can locate a person by what they say. The Bible says in Proverbs 18:21 'Death and life is in the power of the tongue. And they that love it shall eat the fruit of it thereof.' You have to be very careful what you say and what you think. Proverbs 23:7 says 'so as a man thinks in his heart, so is he.' Now I am programming my mind, my time and my attention to get the word of God sown in my heart. Not just in my head. If I get it inside my heart, it's going to be in my mind. Some people have a head faith and they don't get anything from God; but, they don't have a heart faith. That is—faith in the heart!

Faith is a spiritual force. Faith is a force! Faith is an act of power or strength. Faith is a power gift. The Bible says in Hebrews 11 that 'Sara through faith received strength to have a baby at the age of ninety.' Faith is strength! I see myself. And I said before I leave the service tonight, I'm going to command some things in faith and God's going to act on my words. Remember when Elijah said in, 1st Kings 17 'there shall be no rain or dew according to my words.' He didn't say according to God's word. He said my word. Why, because he was a representative of God.

And I'm a representative of God. If I say something, God's got to back it up with his power! I'm a representative of God. I'm an Ambassador of God. I'm a priest of God. I'm an heir of God. I'm one with him. He's one with me. We are living together. He has taken up his abode, his habitation within. I am his temple. You are his temple. We are his dwelling place. We're his tabernacle. We're his building that's made without hands! (Now back to Genesis chapter 32)

FAITH FILLED WORDS

And when he saw that he prevailed not against him, he touched the hallow of his thigh and the hollow of Jacob's thigh was out of joint as he wrestled with him. And he said let me go for the day breaketh. And he said I will not let thee go except thy bless me. (Gen 32:25-26)

The man sad let me go for it is dawn. It hadn't really got quite morning yet. Dawn is the wee-wee hours of the morning. Jacob prevailed. He won! He got the victory! The angel, in the form of a man, said... (Don't miss this. It might be a revelation to some of you.) The angel said, Let me go!

Oh No! Faith won't let go. I don't care how it looks. I don't care how circumstances look. If you believe the word of God then you'll stand in faith and you'll receive the promise of God. You'll hold fast to your confession of your faith without wavering said the Lord. Did not I say in my word, said God, that a double-minded man is unstable in all his ways. That if you doubt, you won't receive anything of the Lord! If you stand in faith and believe the word of God, you'll stand on the promise of God. The promise of God is God's word and God's promise to you.

But a lot of people have not held on to their confession of their faith. They have wavered. They have doubted. They have billowed. You know why they are billowing because of what they say. God done

20

already told them what he is going to do but somebody comes along and tries to make God out of a liar. Or the devil comes along with some deceptive thought. God already gave them a promise. He said speak the word. God is the word. Psalms 33:9 says 'God spoke and it was done. He commanded and it stood fast.'

God had faith filed words. His words were full of faith. When God released his words, faith was being released to those words that caused creation to come into being. Hebrews 11:3 says 'through faith we understand the worlds were framed.' It was framed by what God said—by the word of God. Everything is fashioned and designed and put in its purpose because God spoke his word.

Jacob prevailed, overcame and got the victory because he said something. The angel said let me go! Jacob said 'I will not let thee go! (Faith was talking) except thou bless me.' There comes an exception. You want to go? Then bless me! Then you can go on about your business. God you want me to get out of your face and stop bothering you? Then bless me! I'm not going to stop praying.

ASK! SEEK! KNOCK! 2.1

I'm going to be like that widow woman, avenge me of my adversary! Avenge me of my adversary! Avenge me of my adversary! That unjust judge said, woman you worrying me—come on woman. Just keep coming. You keep knocking at somebody's door. Eventually they will say, stop knocking on my door! Well you go ahead, open up and let me come in then! (cf. Luke 18)

21

You got to be persistent. You got to keep on knocking. I see some of you when you are in prayer. You knock softly, barely, weakly—like maybe nobody's home, we'll just go around the block and leave. No, I will knock! Knock! Knock! And keep on knocking! I can hear God saying: whose knocking on the door like that? You better believe it's me knocking like that because I'm going to make sure you here me.

That's how it is in prayer. Persistency! You got to be about it. You got to be diligent! You got to keep on seeking. You got to keep on asking. You got to keep on knocking! God can hear your prayer. Don't you give up! You stand in faith and believe God. Believe that God will bring his promise to pass in your life. Some of us have been knocking. We been knocking but we've gotten discouraged. We done gave up. We done took down. We've looked at circumstances. But we've lost our persistency. To persist means to continue, to persevere without giving up.

Let's look at that widow woman again. She kept saying judge avenge me of my adversary! The Bible says he was an unjust judge. The man became weary. Liken to your request to God. You can get to a place where God can say oh come on now. I'm tired now—you're coming with the same old request.

Well you go ahead and answer it then! And I'll leave you alone. God is the one who said it. I'm putting God to the test with his word. He said 'command ye me concerning the work of my hands. Remind me. Put me in remembrance of my word.' (cf. Isaiah 43:26) That's what I'm doing when I'm persistent. I'm putting you into remembrance.

22

You're the one who was big enough to say it. You say you are God. Now I'm putting you into remembrance. I've held up my bargain to the word. Now you got to hold to your covenant.

We're in covenant. That's blood on blood. God I'm not coming out of the covenant. God you can't come out of the covenant. God you can't come short of your promise—like when God said he was going to wipe out Israel. He began to bargain with Moses. He told Moses, I'll make you a nation. Moses said, no God. If you wipe out Israel, they will say you brought them out in the wilderness to cut them off and to make you out of a liar. A man got God to change his mind and God repented that he thought the thought in his mind to destroy his people. You can come to the place and the point that God will respect you. God will respect and obey his own word! God will come subject to his word. (cf. Deuteronomy 9)

When I stand in the pulpit and pray for people and desire to see things happen, I don't have to defend God's word. He is the one who said it. If it doesn't happen, that's him. That's his problem, not mine. It's his word not my word. Some of you probably say oh, don't say this about God. But, I don't have to defend the Bible. God will defend his own word because his word is good. God's word is good!

THE ANOINTING

We are still talking about prevailing prayer. We're also talking about persistency and being diligent. We have to be diligent! God rewards diligence. For we know that in Luke18:1 it says, 'he spoke a parable unto them unto this end that men ought always to pray and not faint' Did Jesus say men ought always to gripe, to fuss, to complain, to mumble, to grumble, to get into confusion, to get into unbelief? No. But you find folks doing it: griping, fussing, complaining, arguing and getting into confusion.

And then they wonder why they don't have the power of God operating in their lives. They wonder why they don't have a special anointing to cast out devils and to see miracles happen. You got to get out of that. Some people say that it is impossible for you to live a life without arguing with anybody. No it's not. I live a life without arguing and I'm not perfect. You can pass up some marvelous opportunities to get upset and to get mad. God will pour out a new and a fresh anointing on you—a bucket of anointing!

I was lying down resting tonight before I came to this meeting and God began to talk to me about some anointings. He began to talk to me about the healing anointing; the anointing that comes upon an Intercessor when he prays in the spirit and the anointing for those God has called to stand in certain offices of ministry. Then he gave me Luke 4:18 and said read that son but I said I'm sleepy. I'm tired. I have to read that later. I'm resting my body now. I don't want to read that now. He said 'you remember when Jesus said the spirit of the Lord is upon me because he has anointed me.' The spirit of the Lord came upon him to anoint him to preach the gospel, to set at liberty them that are bruised, to preach recovery of sight to the blind, to heal and bind up the broken hearted. That's what the anointing came upon him for. God anoints people to pray, to intercede.

There is a healing anointing for people to be healed when it's in manifestation and operation. It will be manifested sometime through a person that God has endowed with the gift of healing. Healing can come through the written word of God. You can read the word of God and be healed through the written word of God. You can be healed through the spoken word. You can be healed through a sign, the gift of healing as listed in 1st Corinthians 12.

And he spake a parable unto them to this end that men ought always to pray and not faint. (Luke 18:1) **Don't** be weary in well doing. (Gal. 6:) **B**ut they that wait upon the LORD shall renew their strength; they shall mount up with wings as eagles; they shall run, and not be weary; and they shall walk, and not faint. (Is. 40:31)

While you are running—pray! While you are walking—pray and you won't faint. You won't become weary. You'll be renewed and refreshed when you pray. It'll be like new water when you pray in the spirit of God and build yourself up in the Holy Ghost. Jude has only one chapter and the twentieth verse says 'but ye, beloved, building up yourselves on your most holy faith, praying in the Holy Ghost.' How do you pray in the Holy Ghost? Paul said:

'He that speaks in an unknown tongue speaks not unto men but to God. For if I pray in an unknown tongue, my spirit prays but my mind is unfruitful.' The amplified says unproductive. (cf. 1 Corinthians 14)

Let's look at the word **faint**. A lot of saints are faint-hearted. They are fearful of what they see coming upon the earth, fearful sights, things that are happening in this world. Why, because they are not

25

prevailing in prayer. In Colossians 3:2 God says 'set your affection on things above not on things of this earth.' So many people have their affections set on things on this earth. But I'm setting my face like a flint toward heaven. I'm allowing my spiritual antenna to reach up to God to communicate. I'm not letting a woman, I'm not letting a man, and I'm not letting things, my ministry or nothing keep me from him.

I want something from God! I'm centering my attention on him. I am hungry after God. Deep calleth unto deep! I can hear God saying deep calleth unto deep. I said God I hear it. I hear it! There is a hunger like David says in the word in Psalms 42:1 'as the hart pant's after the brook so does my soul thirst after thee.' Jesus said in Matthew 5:6 'blessed are they which hunger and thirst after righteousness for they shall be filled.'

It's time to get hungry for God. It's time to seek his face evermore. God said he wants to show himself strong and perfect on behalf of those whose heart is perfect toward him. God wants to show him self strong on your behalf. Some people come to church weighted down with the cares of this life. You came to church to sleep. This is no place to sleep. It's time to come alive. It's time to let go of that *spirit of heaviness!* God wants to give you the garments of praise! So you can praise God for that spirit of heaviness. God wants to liberate you and set you free by the power of Almighty God! (cf. Is. 61:3)

God said in Jeremiah 5:14 'my word is going to be like fire in your mouth.' That means people are going to be like wood. And that word is going to consume! God's word is quick. It's sharper than any two-edge sword dividing asunder of soul and spirit, and of the joints

26

and marrow, and is a discerner of the thoughts and intents of the heart. (cf. Hebrews 4:12) That word is alive! That word is the incorruptible seed that's able to bring forth fruit. God wants you to be a fruit bearing Christian. He wants the life of God to come alive in your being!

But you have an enemy like that widow woman who went to that unjust judge which feared not God, neither regarded man: She came unto that judge, saying, Avenge me of mine adversary. The devil is your adversary. He goes about as a roaring lion seeking who he can steal, kill and devour. But I want you to know that the Bible says in the 1st Epistle of John ye are of God, little children, and have overcome them: because greater is he that is in you, than he that is in the world.

PREVAILING PRAYER – GODS LOOKING FOR FAITH
<u>REFLECTION AND STUDY</u>

1. State and write the key scripture in this lesson. Explain the key scripture in your own words.

2. Prayer helps you to manage your emotions and defeat a negative, griping, grumbling and complaining spirit. Prayer helps you to be transformed by the renewing of your mind. Explain this in context of Romans 12:2 and Philippians 2:5:

3. You must not only hear and read the word but you must _____ in _____ to God's word. Walking in obedience to His word is walking in _____.

4. Galatians 6:9 says 'Be not _____ in well doing. You will _____ if you _____ not.' This admonishes us not to give up.

5. Romans 8:31 'If God be for us who can be against us'. To walk in faith you got to _____ the word of God and not walk by _____.

6. According to Isaiah 43:26 Intercessors remind God of what?

7. List some people, places and things Intercessors can lift up in prayer.

8. Define Prevailing prayer?

9. What does the Greek word Nikao mean?

10. How does Webster define victory?

11. Explain how deliverance is wrought by wrestling in prayer? In Genesis 32:24 how does Jacob exhibit wrestling?

13. You can meet with God at 5am or anytime that you set aside to seek his face. Setting aside a special time of prayer and study will help you grow as a Christian.   (True or False)

14. You can hold on to the horns of the altar by fighting the good fight of faith. In 1st John 5:4 _____ is the _____ in everything.

15. How does Elijah in 1st Kings 17 show that faith is strength?

16. Death and life are in the power of the tongue. When Jacob was wrestling with the angel what faith filled words did he say?

17. The word of God tells us in Matthew 7:7 to ask, seek and knock. How does the widow woman in Luke 18 exemplify this pattern?

18. How can you continue this pattern?

19. Some 'anointings' include a healing anointing, anointing to pray. Name some more 'anointings'.

20. What happened to Jesus in Luke 4:18?

PART II

A WINNING SPIRIT!

"God spoke to me and said son: prevailing prayer is that kind of prayer that overcomes and gets the victory. God said son prevailing prayer is prayer that is effective and produces a life line of power with God!"

1.2

God is blessing his people. God is ministering to hearts and lives. I tell you, I'll never be the same. I can literally see what God wants to do in the life of his people by examining my own life. I'm willing to be totally committed to God. I'm willing to sacrifice. I'm willing to pay the price. I'm willing to count up the cost. I said, God I'm willing to be your servant. I'm willing to be your man. We're going to continue talking about prevailing prayer.

We discussed that the word prevail comes from the Greek word **Nikao** and it means to win, to conquer, to overcome, to get the victory. Webster's dictionary says it means to gain superiority over. I read today in Numbers chapter 14 about Joshua and Caleb. They had a different spirit. I have a different spirit. I have a spirit of victory. I don't have a spirit of defeat. I don't have a spirit of doubt. I got a winning spirit. I can't loose bless God. God told Joshua:

'This book of the law shall not depart out of thy mouth but thy shall meditate in it therein day and night. The amplified says you'll be able to, you'll not only have good success but you will deal wisely in all the affairs of life.' (Joshua 1:8)

God wants his people to prosper. In 3rd John chapter 2 God said 'Beloved I wish above all things' (He calls you beloved.) He said 'I wish above all things that thou may prosper and be in good health even as thy soul prospers.' Now that's three-fold prosperity. That's spiritual prosperity, physical prosperity, financial and material prosperity. According to Webster's dictionary the definition of prayer is: The act of asking for a favor with earnestness. A solemn petition for benefits addressed to the Supreme Being; A formula of church service or worship public or private; that part of a petition to a public that specifies a thing desired or granted.

God is a Supreme Being. That's the term that some people call God. Some people say Supreme Being or Higher Power. I like to say GOD! We've been looking at the word Nikao which means to conquer, to overcome or to get the victory—from the Layman's English Greek concordance the word victory. I defined the word victory as the defeat of an enemy in battle.

When you are victorious or you got the victory, you defeat that enemy in battle, in a contest. Or victory is the superiority gained in any contest that's what Webster's Dictionary says. You defeat your enemy. You are a conqueror. Romans 8:37 says 'neigh in all these things we are more than conquerors.' I am a conqueror! I am a victor! I am not bound by sin. I am not a prisoner or a slave to my flesh! I am free! Jesus said in John 8:32 'ye shall know the Truth and the truth shall make you free!'

As we study prevailing prayer, you're going to see that prevailing prayer has an effect upon our inward man. I'm seeing tremendous results in my home, in my life. I'm seeing God put things together. The devil's fighting. He can do what he wants to do. I'm not giving him any praise. I'm not giving him any glory. I'm giving the praise, the honor and the glory to God because I thank God that I pray! Prayer is communication with God. Prayer is fellowshipping with God. We need to be intimate with God. We need to take time that quiet time alone and get in a secret place.

I can show you Jesus in prayer in Mark 1:35 when he went out to a solitary place—a place of solitude. He was alone, by himself. Like I go into that closet every night to get alone with God so that God can talk to me about the needs of his people. I told you that God wants to meet with you. Like in Exodus 19 God said to Moses 'bring the people out of the camp so they can meet with me.' But you can't meet with God until number one: You wash your clothes! And number two: Sanctify yourself! God wants us to meet with him.

DON'T TALK DEFEAT

Prevailing in prayer has an effect upon our inward man. Prevailing in prayer produces tremendous results as it did for Jacob in Genesis 32. Jacob prevailed with God. He overcame. He won. He got the victory! He didn't give in and give up because he didn't get an immediate answer or an instantaneous answer to his petition. God changed his name to Israel. Israel means he struggles with God. Jacob means supplanter.

Prevailing in prayer produces tremendous results. We will see amazing answers to our prayers. Prevailing prayer is that kind of prayer that overcomes and conquers. Now I was in prayer and God gave me what I'm reading to you. I didn't get this out of a textbook. The spirit of God gave this to me and I wrote it down. God spoke to me and said: Son, prevailing prayer is that kind of prayer that overcomes and gets the victory. God said 'son prevailing prayer is that prayer that is effective and produces a life line of power with God.' Jacob had power with God and with men. You can find favor with God in prayer. You can have power with God. I'm not bragging but I have power with God and I know it! I have power with God and I have found favor with man because I have prevailed in prayer.

Prevailing prayer is that kind of prayer that produces power with God who is a person. Let us now study that we might have power with God. Now this is a lesson. I taught this lesson when I was Pastor of a church. We said Vision of Faith. But it's no longer Vision of Faith. We do have a vision and it has to be of faith… Prayer is joining forces with God the Father. It is fellowship with him. Prayer is communion with God who is a person. God wants his people to overcome. God wants his people to get the victory.

> 'And Jacob was left alone and there wrestled a man with him until the breaking of the day. When he saw that he prevailed' (Genesis 3:24)

34

Again we emphasize on that word prevail because we're talking about prevailing prayer. Your Bible is your textbook so you mark that word in your Bible. Get you a Bible that you can mark in. I look up words. I study them and I mark it in my Bible. I am a student of the word of God. I refuse to be an ignoramus! God said in:

> Hosea 4:6 'my people are destroyed or they perish for a lack of knowledge. (Isaiah 5:19) they go into exile—they go into captivity for a lack of knowledge.'

People are deceived, confused and messed up because they don't study to show themselves approved unto God to be workmen. You got people running from church to church. They don't know what's in the Bible. They don't know if that preacher's telling them a lie or telling the truth. Bring your Bible to church with you. I don't want you to miss it. God doesn't want you going to hell over some man's mistake. Some of us done put the stake to the midst…

POWER WITH GOD

> 'When he saw that he prevailed not against him, he touched the hallow of his thigh and the hallow of Jacob's thigh was out of joint as he wrestled with him.' (Genesis 32:25)

Let's look at the word wrestle in that particular verse. Wrestling denotes strenuous effort. It's a struggle going on here, a confrontation: 'And he said let me go (this is the angel speaking) for the day breaketh. And he said I will not let thee go.' (Genesis 32:26) When you want something from God you can't let him go. You can't get up. I know I don't get off of my knees until I know I got the victory. I'm in prayer every day. I don't walk out of that place or leave that church until I know I got an answer from God. And I know that I got an answer when I start laughing. I begin to sing. That's why I come in here and praise God. I can't just be bound up. Praise breaks the chains that have you bound. The word of God says:

> 'Offer unto God the sacrifice of praise the fruit of our lips giving thanks unto his name.' (Hebrews 13:15)
> David said 'I will bless the Lord at all times and his praise shall continually be in my mouth.' (Psalms 34:1)

God inhabits the praises of Israel. God brought his people out when they began to praise him and when they began to lift up his name. Let's talk about the power of praise. There is power behind praise. Praise brings deliverance. Ask Paul and Silas when they were in that jail at about midnight. Jacob was wrestling with this angel too about midnight. Something's always going on at midnight. Some of you folks are in the bed sleep. You go to bed too early. You never see an angel come out. You're always in the bed. Some folks are not in the bed, but they're watching television and God is trying to talk to them. God wants to speak to you. You need to turn that television off and get into a place of prayer and let God talk to you.

I don't find myself always running up into prayer lines and letting preachers prophesy and tell me what God said. I get on my face and let God tell me what he wants me to say. I'm not running to this meeting and to that meeting to get that preacher or to get that minister to lay his hands on me. I'll let Jesus lay his hands on me.

> 'And he said unto them what is thy name. He said Jacob. Thou name shall no more be called Jacob but Israel, God's people.' (Genesis 32:27-28)

36

God raised up a nation out of the new name that he gave Jacob. 'For as a prince has thou power with God and with men.' When you got power with God, you're going to have power with men. How did Jacob come into this revelation of power or authority? Through prayer, not letting go, not giving up and prevailing. Refusing to quit! Refusing to take down and refusing to look at circumstances! So many of us, we magnify our circumstances and situations instead of magnifying the word. But David said 'for thou hast magnified thy word above all thy name.' (Ps. 138:2)

Some people are hung up on the name of Jesus. I love the name of Jesus. It's precious and sweet but the name apart from the word won't do you a bit of good. The Sons of Sceva they had the name. But they didn't have the knowledge and power of the word. (cf. Acts 19)

That name is just like a power of attorney, but that name has to be given to you. For example, you can't just take my name and go and do anything you want with it. You have to have my signature before you can do anything with the things that belong to me. If a person writes a check, that check will be void. It won't be any good until you have their signature on the check. That's just the way it is.

SEEKING GODS FACE

'Thou name shall no more be called Jacob but Israel: for as a prince hast thou power with God and with men, and hast prevailed.' Mark the word **prevail** again. We saw it in the 25th verse and now we see it in the 28th verse. 'And Jacob asked him, and said, tell me, I pray thee, thy name. And he said, wherefore is it that thou dost ask after my name? And he blessed him there. And Jacob called the name of the place Peniel: for I have seen God face to face and my life is preserved.' (Genesis 32:28-30)

That word **Peniel** means I've seen God face to face. For, I have seen God face to face and my life is preserved. You can see God face to face by spending time with him in prayer. God will reveal himself to you. If you spend much time with him in prayer you can grow up. You can be what God will have you to be. You can not find a great ministry or a great man or woman. It comes through much travail and prevail and much intercession because you got to die to yourself.

Luke 9: 23 says 'and he said to them all, If any man will come after me, let him deny himself, and take up his cross daily, and follow me.' That's a life. That's the life that Jesus lived. The cross is the life that he lived. Take up thy cross and follow me. Take up your cross and follow me. What? The life that I'm living, let's go, come on. Let's walk! Everybody wants a crown but nobody wants to carry a cross. You got people saying we shall wear a golden crown but have you picked up a cross yet? Have you carried the cross yet? No cross, no crown. Christ carried his cross. The very cross that he carried, they buried him on it. They hung him on it, crucified him on it. Put him to death. Paul said I'm crucified with Christ. Paul was letting the people know that I'm carrying a cross. He even said in Galatians 6:17 'from henceforth let no man trouble me, for I bear in my body the marks.'

I can say with the Apostle Paul don't let no man trouble me because I bear in my body the marks of the Lord Jesus Christ. I am his chosen servant. There is a seal. Every person that God calls and he qualifies for the ministry there is a seal on them. They're marked. God's people are stamped with the seal of redemption. The seal is the Holy Spirit. He seals us until the day of redemption. God is so much in love with his people that he's trying to bring us to the place and to the point that we can receive the revelation of the word.

Tradition makes the word of God of none affect. You can't see this type of power demonstrated through traditional religious beliefs. You got to throw your tradition and religion in the garbage and pick up the power of God. I threw tradition and religion in the garbage. It wasn't any good. It hindered Jesus from what he wanted to do. *He said how come ye marvel?* He was trying to do many and mighty works in his home town but he couldn't for he marveled at the unbelief of the people. (cf. Mark 6:6)

The people said, oh that's just brother Jesus—that's just Mary and Joseph's boy. Jesus said a prophet is not honored in his own town and among his own kin. He's not honored in his own town and among his own kin but everywhere else he is honored. (See Mark 6:4) He's respected. Jesus considered himself a Prophet, an Apostle—the High Priest of our confession. Jesus was an Evangelist. He said I must preach the gospel where also I am sent. That's an Evangelist. Jesus was a Pastor. He said I am the Good Shepherd of the sheep.

Jesus was a Teacher. (cf. John 10) He came to teach the word of God. You find Jesus teaching, preaching and healing. Jesus stood in the five-fold ministry. He was an Apostle—a sent one of God. He was a Prophet—a Spokesman for God. He was a Pastor, a Shepherd that had the heartbeat of God for the sheep. He was an Evangelist. He preached the gospel. He went from place to place traveling, preaching the gospel. And he was a Teacher of God's word. He came to teach people the Truth's of God. Jesus Christ the son of God, he had power with God.

Jesus knew the power of prayer. He did much of it in his day and his time. I find Jesus casting out devils, performing miracles and teaching the word of God during the day but at night, I find him in a solitary place all night in prayer with God. I find Jesus spending time in prayer with God. He taught his disciples how to pray.

PRAYING IN POWER

You want power with God and you want to be a success in the ministry. You want to be successful. You want to achieve and advance. Then, seek my face said the Lord. Seek me while I may be found. Call upon me while I am near. (cf. Is. 55:6) You want to prosper. You want to be successful but seek ye first the kingdom of God and my righteousness and all these things will be added unto you. (cf. Mt. 6:33) God says Oh yes, I desire to bless my people. I desire to cause my people to prosper. I desire to see my people successful. 'I delight in the prosperity of my servant.' (Psalms 35) God loves to see me blessed. One day I may walk in here with a gold suit on. God loves to see his servants prosper. He wants to see all of us prosper.

> 'And as he passed over Penuel the sun rose upon him, and he
> halted upon his thigh. Therefore the children of Israel eat not
> of the sinew which shrank, which is upon the hollow of the
> thigh, unto this day: because he touched the hollow of Jacob's
> thigh in the sinew that shrank.' (Gen 32:31-32)

We see Jacob prevailing, winning, overcoming, and getting the victory. Not giving up wherein the angel said let me go. Jacob said I will not let thee go. I can see a child of God saying I'm not getting up off of my knees Lord until you do it.

In Luke 18:1 Jesus 'spoke a parable unto them to this end that men ought always to pray and not faint.' When you find people fainting, they are not praying. Jesus said to his disciples could you not watch with me one hour? They were asleep! Sometimes when I go to church, I am so tired and fatigued. But when I get in prayer and get into intercession and begin to pray in tongues, I'm not so tired. I'm not tired tonight. I went home last night and rested. I rested today and I got up and made it to the church at twelve o'clock noon. I was in Intercessory prayer. I love prayer. It's my language. Prayer is my talk. I am refreshed!

Jude has only one chapter and the 20th verse says 'but ye, beloved, building up yourselves on your most holy faith, praying in the Holy Ghost.' Sort of like when your building up a car battery. The scripture says 'building yourselves up on your most holy faith praying in the Holy Ghost.' How do you pray in the Holy Ghost? Paul said 'if I speak with an unknown tongue my spirit prays but my mind is unfruitful.' The amplified says unproductive. When you pray with your spirit, you are praying with tongues. 'This is the hour that the true worshippers shall worship the Father in spirit and in truth; for the father seeks such to worship Him.' (John 4:23)

If you get a lot of word of God inside of people they won't live in sin because John says you have this seed remaining in you and you cannot sin. He didn't say you would not sin. He said you could not sin. David said thy word have I hid in my heart that I might not sin against thee. He had the word in his heart but he still committed adultery with

Bathsheba. He took another man's wife and had him murdered. Yet David said:

> 'Thy word have I hidden in mine heart, that I might not sin against thee.' 'The entrance of thy words giveth light; it giveth understanding unto the simple.' 'Forever oh Lord, thy word is settled in heaven.' 'Thy word is a light unto my path and a lamp unto my feet.' (Psalms 119:11, 130, 89, 105)

I'm not trying to impress anybody by how much scripture I can quote. I'm full of the word of God. Jesus said in Matthew 5:6 'blessed are they that hunger and thirst for righteousness, for they shall be filled.' I'm filled with it! Glory be to God! It's flowing out of my belly!

THE VOICE OF GOD

Some of you are filled with the wrong thing. You're filled with foolishness! You're filled with doubt! You're filled with unbelief! You're filled with strife, bitterness and jealousy. We need to be filled with God's love. God has spoken to me and told me to read 1st Corinthians the thirteenth chapter everyday. So when I get up, before I talk to anybody, I read 1st Corinthians chapter thirteen everyday and every night. I want the God kind of love—the agape love of God to be manifested on the inside of my being. My desire is to be like Jesus. God spoke to me and I heard it out there one night in the parking lot and a brother confirmed what God had said to me on last night.

When people come up to me and prophesy, I don't care who it is, if they come up to me and tell me what God says and I know it's a lie, I don't have to say that they are lying. I know they are lying because I know the voice of God for myself.

God speaks by a voice. We showed you that last night in Exodus 19. God has a voice and he does speak. But can you distinguish His voice? What voice is talking to you? What voice is telling you to do this and it will be alright? Is that the voice of God or the voice of the enemy? Satan has a voice and he is deceiving preachers and he's deceiving God's people. He'll deceive a preacher to deceive the people of God.

We see that God has a voice. 1st Kings, chapter 19 says the Lord was not in the earthquake. The Lord was not in the fire. The Lord was not in the wind but he was in a still small voice. Psalms 46:10 says 'be still and know that I am God.' You got to get in a quiet place like Jacob did and wrestle. Wrestling denotes strenuous effort.

You're agonizing of the soul. When a person is praying they are agonizing of the soul. (cf. Luke 22:44) Your soul consists of your mind, your emotions and your will. You wonder how come people get into the flesh and fall into sin. They fall back, even preachers falling down. Why? Because they don't spend that time with God in Intercessory prayer! Letting the flesh die! Paul said I die daily! (See 1st Cor. 15:31) You're having a problem with the flesh? You can overcome! I had a problem with the flesh but I overcame. You can overcome.

PREVAILING PRAYER – A WINNING SPIRIT
REFLECTION AND STUDY

1. The Greek word _____ means to win, to conquer, to overcome, to get the victory.

2. In reference to a winning spirit Numbers 14 says that _____ and_____ were of a different spirit. They did not have a _____ mentality. They were well able to overcome who?

3. What does Joshua 1:8 say about success? In 3rd John 2 what does it say about prosperity?

4. State in your own words the definition of prayer. Compare it to Webster.

5. Victory is the _____ of an enemy in _____.

6. According to Webster Victory is:

7. According to Romans 8:37 we are _____.

8. In Mark 1:35 what kind of prayer do we find Jesus in?

9. In Exodus 19 God wanted Moses to bring the people out for what?

10. In Genesis 32 what produced a lifeline of power with God?

11. Is praise a weapon? How did praise bring deliverance for Paul and Silas in Acts 16?

12. Can a person magnify their circumstances over the word of God?

13. Who in Acts 19 showed that you need more than the name of Jesus? Why? How is Power of Attorney over someone and example?

14. The word Peniel means-

15. Luke 9:23 says if any man shall come after me let him deny who?

16. Great ministries and great men and women of God spend much time with God in intercessory prayer letting the _____ die.

17. How does tradition hinder spiritual growth? (See pg. 44)

18. Did Jesus function in all areas of the five-fold ministry?

19. Isaiah 5:6 says to _____ God's face. Matthew 6:33 says to seek first the kingdom of God and what else?

20. In reference to Luke 18:1, when you find people fainting they are not _____.

21. Intercession consists of praying in _____ as spoken of in Jude 20.

22. John 4:23 says God wants us to worship in _____ and in _____.

23. What verses in Ps 119 tell us about how important God's word is?

24: Jesus said in Matt. 5:6 'blessed are they that hunger and _____ for _____ sake for they shall be filled'. If you're filled with God's word you won't be filled with the wrong thing such as doubt, unbelief, s_____, b_____ and jealousy.

25. How do you know if the voice that is talking to you is God's voice, your own voice or the voice of the enemy?

26. Satan's voice deceives people. In 1st Kings 19 how did God speak? What does Ps 46:10 say?

26. Your soul consists of your _____, emotions and your will.

27. Luke 22:44 speaks of agonizing of the soul. That's how you overcome the _____.

28: In 1st Corinthians 15:31 the Paul said I die _____.

29. When you spend time in intercession with God you die to the _____ and you want fall back into sin.

PART III

THE SUPERNATURAL

"The Lord told me, he said son I want you to think victory. I want you to walk prosperity. I want you to live it. I want you to sleep it and I want you to eat it!"

Jesus said according to your faith be it unto you. He said 'if thou canst believe, all things are possible to him that believeth.' (Mark 9:23) He said with men things may be impossible but with God all things are possible. With your faith you are a conqueror! You are a victor! You are not a victim but you are a victor! You need to walk like a victor. You need to talk like a victor! You need to live like a victor! You need to live like an heir of God. You say my God supplies all of my needs according to his riches and glory. Your job is not your source. Your pastor is not your source. Your wife is not your source! Your husband is not your source! God is your source! (cf. Phil. 4:19)

The Apostle Paul said those whom the Lord has ordained shall be supplied by the gospel they preach. (cf. 1 Cor. 9:14) God said that he has pleasure and he delights in the prosperity of his servant. God's able to take care of his own. He took care of the man Elijah. God sent Elijah to the brook Cherith. When the brook dried up, God said I want you to go to Zarephath. I got a widow woman. God's always got a woman to take care of his man whom he has placed and anointed. When God has placed the call of God on a man's life, God's always got a woman.

Not only does he have a woman, he has a raven. God said I command the ravens to feed you. I command that widow woman to sustain you. The man of God had to teach her how to give to God first. When she gave to the man of God, she was giving to God because that was God's servant. Elijah the Prophet said to that widow woman:

> 'If ye bake me thereof a little cake first, and bring it unto me, and after make for thee and for thy son. For thus saith the LORD God of Israel, The barrel of meal shall not waste, neither shall the cruse of oil fail, until the day that the LORD sendeth rain upon the earth. And she went and did according to the saying of Elijah: and she, and he, and her house, did eat many days.' (See 1 Kings 17:1-16)

Afterwards, that woman said, now I know the word of the Lord in thy mouth is true. Why, because he was a man of God. God's got a plan and God's got a man. And he's got a purpose. All those needs are met. The Lord told me, he said, 'son I want you to think victory. I want you to walk prosperity. I want you to live it. I want you to sleep it and I want you to eat it!' People are going to talk. They are going to talk if you got something. They are going to talk if you don't have anything. They are going to talk if you preach like Paul or cast out devils like Peter. They are going to talk.

But I refused to eat the crumbs of the loaves when God wants me to have the whole loaf. We are *heirs and priest of God.* (cf. Rom.

8:17, Rev. 1:6) We are a peculiar people. We are of a royal family! God said he owns a thousand cattle on a hill. (cf. Ps 50:10) He said I have ten-thousand blessings in my right hand to satisfy the poor. God said all the gold and the silver is mine. The Bible says in Psalm 24:1 'the earth is the Lord's and the fullness thereof and they that dwelleth therein.' The anointing is wide open. *(Relating to the loudness of the microphone)* The anointing is down on the inside of me. I preached downtown Miami for years without a microphone!

It is time to prevail and overcome! We been minimized and mesmerized by the devil. Satan has said some ugly things about the church. The words that he spoke, the devil is going to eat. He's going to eat them ugly words. The devil said we'll never be what God wants us to be. The devil said we'll never be blessed. But God has brought us out into a good land. We've already possessed it. Some of us can't possess it because of what were confessing. We profess one thing and we confess another. Let your profession be your confession. What you profess—confess. If you profess your needs are met, then confess your needs are met.

SPEAK THE WORD

Stop saying, oh how are we going to pay the bills. How are we going to do this? You're looking at how you are going to do it. You're not depending on your source, your source of supply. I don't worry about how I'm going to turn the lights on. I just put a bulb in it and turn it on. I turn the power on and it comes on.

Do your faith like that. Turn your faith on like you turn that switch on. Turn your faith on! Release your faith! Release your faith! Turn your faith on like the flick of a switch! Turn it on! Like Brother Hagan say: Turn it loose! I dare you to believe God's word. I dare you to put your faith to work. James said you show me your faith without your works (your actions) and I'll show you my faith by my works (which is my actions.) (See James 2:14-26) If you have faith in God, you're going to walk on his word. You're going to stand and believe. You don't have to see it.

Like Elijah the man of God. *(They were cutting down trees in the woods)* A little boy had borrowed an axe-head. That axe head fell in the water. And the little boy said: oh man of God! Oh man of God! You know little school boys. They're always getting into trouble. He had borrowed the axe-head. And he cried: it's borrowed! It's borrowed! The axe-head had fallen in that water. The man of God came and stood there. And the man of God spoke the words of faith out of his mouth and commanded that thing to come up out of there. That axe surfaced out of the water. That axe surfaced out of the water at the words of a man! (See 2 Kings 6)

Jesus defied the laws of nature. He didn't walk on the water as the son of God. He did it as the son of man. Some people say he did it as God, but no, he did not. Jesus used the gift of faith. He used the gift of faith and the gift of the working of miracles to defy the laws of nature. He did it as the son of man. He raised the dead as the son of man. I read John 14:12 often. Jesus said 'he that believeth on me the works that I do' (I believe on him. Don't you believe on him?) He said 'he that believeth on me the works that I do, shall he do also.' (Shall he or she, who? The one that believes on him) Do you believe on him? 'He that believeth on me and the works that I do, shall he do even greater works than these.'

Jesus never preached to a multitude on the radio. Jesus never had a television broadcast ministry. He never had *Jesus Christ Ministries*. Jesus never walked the streets with a briefcase. "Alright, that's Brother Jesus!" "And now that's Brother Jesus!" I'm not making fun of him. I'm just showing you something. He said we will do greater than what he did.

For example, in a service one night, I said to the people: I'm not going to touch you. I'm going to walk by you and God's going to begin to touch you. And when I walked by them people began to fall. I didn't touch them or lay hands on them. Peter did it. Jesus never seen 5,000 people come to his ministry. Jesus never had anyone saved up under his ministry. In his entire work of God, in the four gospels, I never found Jesus praying for the sick. He just laid hands on them and healed them. He said 'these signs shall follow them that believe. In my name they shall lay hands on the sick and they shall recover.' He didn't say pray for them. He said lay hands on them. Then he sent his disciples out. He didn't tell them to pray for the sick. He said heal the sick. He didn't say go and get a coffin and bury the dead. He said, raise the dead! Cleanse the lepers! Cast out devils! (cf. Mark 16:17)

I'm just a Jesus preacher. Some people say I talk more about Jesus than I do anything else, but I'm just a Jesus preacher and that's all. If I don't know anything else all I know is what Jesus taught me to say. I believe in casting out devils. That's fun! It's an honor. Glory to God! If you have the knowledge of the power of God and if you have the knowledge of the power of God that is on the inside of you: If you get into some type of sin, you can cast the devil out of yourself. You can get yourself free.

Some people are bound. And they say, "Apostle Martin, I can't get free from this thing. You want to call up Brother Martin, I might be somewhere in New York City. You might be at death's door. You can call on Jesus and he will answer your prayer just like he will answer my prayer. You don't need Apostle Martin to lay his hands on you. Lay your hands on yourself! We want the preacher to do everything. We want to look to a man and get a confirmation from a man when we ought to look to God's word. Look to Jesus! Jesus can give you what you need.

WHOSE POWER IS IT?

For three nights, in these services, God hasn't let me lay hands on anybody. I just minister the word. When I'm finished, I get into the car and go home. You have probably said he doesn't really talk. He hardly communicates. When service is over, he's just gone and he don't lay hands. He didn't pray with anybody.

Why? Because God said, son, what my people need is my word. Not (your so called) you trying to build your ministry up and make folks think you got the power. Deliverance and power is in his word. You deceive people when you build yourself up. You get yourself into trouble with God. You get a big head. You get a swell head and nobody can tell you anything. I don't want to get a swell head. The honor and the glory belongs' to God, where it belongs!

Some of us think we're doing it. We think we've got the power to deliver people. And we say: if they don't come to me and I don't lay my hands on them they won't get it. But that's a lie! You are not Jesus! I don't have to lay my hands on you for God to give you a miracle. You can get down on your knees and get a miracle in prayer!

Like I told that sister at the church one-day, I said: you don't need Sister Joyce or anybody else to lay hands on you. Jesus will touch you if you need a miracle from him. God is not going to allow any flesh, me or anybody else, to take his glory. 'No man, no flesh shall glory in the presence of Almighty God.' It is well said. That keeps us humble. (cf. 1 Corinthians 1:29)

We have to realize that God is performing these miracles. Sometimes God begins to work and do things through you and you think you're doing it. I'm talking to myself too because the devil will really try to get you lifted up. And when you get lifted up no-one can tell you anything. We want to remain humble. We want to remain meek and lowly and realize that it is God's miracle working power. Let's give the credit to him. Let's give the glory to God. Let's give all the honor and the power to him.

FLOW WITH THE ANOINTING

It's just five minutes after ten and God said: son stop right now—I'm going to obey the spirit of God. I have no anointing on me now to lay hands on anybody but I can come and pray for you in faith. I understand what God is doing. He's not going to let anybody take his glory. Lord I don't want your glory. And I thank you Lord.

Many nights, if he doesn't let me lay my hands on anybody until the entire meeting is over, then that's fine with me. I'm not telling Jesus what to do. I don't want his glory. It doesn't belong to me. And I'm obeying the spirit of God. I'm not going to get in the flesh and try to lay hands on you. There's no anointing there.

Sometimes when the anointing is in my hand they begin to sweat but there's no anointing there right now. As I said, I can pray for you in faith but there is no anointing. I like to do it when the spirit of God anoints me. I feel like a mighty man when the anointing is there and you get better results. When the anointing is not there, it's just not there.

Somebody came into one of my meetings once and said he's scared to lay hands on me. And I said no I'm not. I'm led by the spirit of God. If you want prayer, I'll ask Minister Blacks if he would like to do so. He can come and pray for you. He might have an anointing on him to pray for you. I am serious about ministry. I have to flow with the spirit of God. I flow with the anointing of God. I don't get into the flesh.

I flow with the anointing because the moment you start walking in error and start doing things on your own, you miss God. You deceive people and you hurt people. I'm learning how to be obedient and how to be led by the spirit. And sometimes God will make allowance for you, as you go along and minister. He'll be teaching you so you don't think your doing it. Because you could start laying hands on people and when they start falling out under the power, you'll think you're doing it and you get yourself into trouble.

That almost happened to me one time. The devil will get you tripped up if you let him. He will have you running around with your chest all stuck out. You got your head up thinking: I'm somebody now! I see people falling down under the power. Everybody I touch fall up under the power. You get big headed. You get yourself in trouble and get deceived and then you start teaching erroneous doctrine. You start making up your own little cliché's about what the word of God says and you have no anointing behind it. God said son, I'm not going to allow you or anyone else to take my glory.

God keep telling me this, he said remember the servant can become as his master but the servant is not greater than his Lord. That's what you call greatness there. When you recognized that you can be real great. When you're open, when you're honest and when you're sincere with people because I don't want to miss it. If I do miss it say Lord bless him and help him to get back on the right track. I don't want to be in error. I don't want to deceive God's people. God wants you to be blessed! You need to lift up the men and women of God and pray for us. We need your prayers because we're not perfect and we've got the devil to contend with just like you do.

It's just seven minutes after ten. I love you and most of all God loves you. How many were here one night when I used the mantle of the Lord? The anointing of God was in my jacket, in my coat. The anointing of God is in my coat tonight. I feel it right now as I hold it in my right hand. So I'm going to pray for you. *Apostle Martin calls a woman up. He begins to minister to her:*

PRAYER FOR A WOMAN
WHO'S SON IS SICK

Miss do you know somebody that is sick? What's wrong with your son? He is sick on crack she responds. Miss, are you married? Is your husband a born again Christian? God wants to save your husband. Miss, I'm going to do something that might not seem very nice to you but I'm going to do this like the Lord told me to do it. Hold your hands out. I'm going to throw this coat to you and the power of God is going to come on you as a sign unto you and as a sign unto this congregation that the Lord spoke to me and that what I'm telling you is directly from the Lord.

Miss, open your eyes and catch my coat! Now close your eyes and hold it with both of your hands. God is touching you right now. God's power is all over you. Jesus is touching you right now! God is touching you, liberating you and liberating your mind. He is giving you peace right now. There it is. That's God power all over you. As you hold that mantle in your hands, that's the power of God just relax right now. Let him bless and touch you. There it is. She's drawing from that anointing. Look at the peace of God coming on her now...

PRAYER FOR A WOMAN
RELUCTANT TO COME FORTH

Come here sister. Tell that sister right there to come here. You! That sister right there! Come on daughter. You! No, her! She is pointing at everybody else and I'm talking to her. God is doing something in you sister. It's a work. He hasn't fully completed it but he wants to complete it. I want you to stand right there sister. Close your eyes and lift up both of your hands. (She does so as reluctantly as she came forward) I'm going to break the power of the devil off of you tonight! Somebody is trying to work witchcraft on you. You have a fear—a tormenting type of fear. It's not from God but it's from the devil. Sister I want you to say this with me right now:

Say, "In Jesus name I declare my liberty!" There it is. Hold this mantle in your hands sister. That's your liberty. The spirit of God is liberating you right now from the crown of your head to the soles of your feet. That's God's power coming on you sister liberating you. That's the anointing of God from that mantle right there. There it is. Sister God has been dealing with you about something. You know what it is. He told me that you know what it is. God's been dealing with you. The Lord says sister he wants you to be obedient and to do what he is asking you to do. And God is going to bless you. God's touching you right now...

PRAYER FOR A CHILD

Father in Jesus name, God I pray for this little daughter. Lord I ask you to bless her and God I ask you to touch her in the name of Jesus. From the crown of her head to the soles of her feet let her be blessed in Jesus name. Amen. Isn't that sweet? We're not going to turn that little baby away.

DEMONS CAST OUT OF A YOUNG LADY

This sister right here! You! I wanted to get to you the other night but I forgot it and when I got home the Spirit of God—God kind of got on to me because I had forgot about it. My sister, are you born again? You're not born again right? You know Jesus loves you right? And you know that he died on the cross for your sins right?

Let me ask you something. Are you from Miami? Are you from here? Where are you from? You're from Lake City, Florida. Are you visiting here? You live here now right. I see a lot of hurt. I see confusion. I see you—you been ruffed up a little bit. I'm not here to embarrass you publicly. I'm not here to hurt you. I'm here because I'm concerned about you. Most of all God loves you young lady. Jesus loves you. Praise God. I don't know who has—what you have been through—the hurt, the pain that this person has caused you. But I want to let you know in the midst of it all God loves you. Jesus loves you too. Praise God.

Let me ask you something. Are you married? You're not married. Do you have a baby? You have three children. Thank you Jesus! Miss, God loves you. God loves you and he loves your little daughter right there too. Praise God. I just want you to raise both of your hands. Close your eyes and I'm going to pray a prayer and I want you to repeat this prayer after me right now. (She repeats after him.)

Just say with me, Jesus I repent and I confess of all my sins with my mouth. I confess Jesus Christ as my Lord and my Savior. In my heart I believe that God has raised Jesus Christ from the dead. Lord Jesus come into my heart! Come in today. Come in to stay. Satan! I resist you! And I renounce you! Devil! I will no longer (her voice is broken up and she begins to cry out oh! Oh! Lord Jesus save my soul!) Don't let her hurt herself brother! (She falls to the floor and you hear screams, shrieks and hollers. In the midst of her conversion, Elder Peterson says God is good.)

How many believe I'm obedient to the spirit of God. That's why I had to say what I had to say because I can't be disobedient. You see the other night I wasn't supposed to do that but I was supposed to talk to her but I didn't. But tonight God said if you do it tonight, I'm going to spank you when you get home. No, not tonight! God's not going to spank me when I get home. Praise God. I'm going to obey God.

Someone might ask, why didn't you tell her about leading her to the Lord? I couldn't do that. I had to use the wisdom of God. Sometimes when you're fishing, you got to be wise. You just say let's pray this prayer. You know how they play when they get you out in the world. They won't really tell you what's going on. They will be slick about it. So we got to kind of know how to fish a little bit. Sneak a fish in. Wow! What a great catch! Hallelujah! Wow! Can you say amen! Isn't that beautiful! Isn't that wonderful! All heaven is rejoicing! Come on let's rejoice saints. How many believe God's blessing her. Thank you Jesus! Minister Blacks just lay your hand on her. The enemy has been trying to oppress this sister. Just take authority over the devil:

Father in the name of Jesus! We bind every oppressing spirit. Now Satan you don't have no more legal right. This young lady has surrendered herself unto the Lord Savior Jesus Christ. And we bind your work. And we command you to stop right now! We command you to stop! (Tongues)

Stop! Your maneuvers against her mind, against her body, against her will. Come out of her! That's it right there. Come out of her! Let her go! We decree victory! We decree deliverance! (Tongues) (Ooooooogggh, screeches and cries can be heard) Come out of her in Jesus name! Come out! Come out of her now! (Repeated) I bind you in Jesus name and I command you to come out. (Repeated) In the name of Jesus! You say what are they doing? We are casting out spirits. That's it she's free! Give God the praise. The girl is free! …

PREVAILING PRAYER – THE SUPERNATURAL
<u>REFLECTION AND STUDY</u>

1. In Mark 9:23 what does Jesus say about belief?

2. God is your source. What does Phil. 4:19 say about your needs?

3. In 1st Cor. 9:14 how does God supply the needs of those ordained?

4. In 1st Kings 17:1-16 how did God take care of Elijah?

5. How was God teaching the widow woman faith for her needs?

6. According to Romans 8:17 and Rev. 1:6 we are heirs and _____ of God.

7. Discuss Faith versus works as relayed in James 2:14-26.

8. God is also teaching us faith. Do you agree that we must confess faith, stop worrying and make positive faith filled confessions?

9. Is faith a gift?

10. How did Jesus walk in the gift of faith?

11. According to John 14:12 what did he say that we can do?

12. What did he commission his disciples to do in Mark 16:17?

13. As a disciple of Jesus, do you believe you have power?

14. Discuss what he said about casting out demons and devils?

15. The power belongs to God. God's power flows through us so no man shall glory in his _____. (1 Cor. 1:29)

16. Discuss flowing with the anointing in comparison to operating in the flesh.

17. Have you ever witnessed the supernatural?

18. How has God taught you faith and how have you personally operated in the gift of faith?

INTERCESSORY PRAYER

PART I

WATCHMAN ON THE WALL

"We've got more people feasting that they are fasting. We've got more people playing than they are praying. God's looking for Intercessors who will be Watchmen!"

'We know not what we should pray for as we ought but the spirit itself maketh intercession for us with groanings which can not be uttered. And he that searcheth the hearts knows what is the mind of the spirit because he maketh intercession for the saints according to the will of God.' (Romans 8:.26, 27)

3.1

An Intercessor is one who takes the place of another. An Intercessor is one who pleads another's case. That's what an Intercessor is, somebody going before someone else representing you. Prayer is communication with God. Prayer is joining forces with God who is our Father. Prayer is fellowshipping with God.

Amplified version, so to the Holy Spirit comes to our aid. Somebody that aides you, they are helping you. They're supporting you—likewise as we ask for your assistance to us in our endeavor to fulfill the call of God and the commission of God. You make it possible, through your gifts and support.

> (Romans 8:26) 'so to the Holy Spirit comes to your aid and bears us up in our weakness. For we do not know what prayer to offer nor how to offer it worthily as we ought. But the Spirit himself'

(I like this translation) goes to meet our supplication and pleads in our behalf with unspeakable yearnings, that's groaning. What is an unspeakable yearning? It's something too deep for words to utter. You can't speak that. Sometimes when people are in prayer, you hear groaning. You say, what did they say? It's an unspeakable yearning, too deep for words to utter. You can't put it into words. It's too inexpressible to speak in words.

> Vs 27 'and he that searcheth the hearts knoweth what is the mind of the Spirit, because he maketh intercession for the saints according to the will of God.'

You mean to tell me that the Holy Spirit has a mind? Yes he does. The Holy Spirit thinks like God. The Holy Spirit is God. He is the Spirit of God. He is the Glory of God. He's the power of God. 'So to the Holy Spirit comes to your aid and bears us up.'(AB) He's bearing you! He's holding you up. He's not doing your praying for you. He's aiding you. He's supporting you. He's helping you. He's not going to pray for you. He's going to accompany and assist you in your praying. That's the work of the Holy Spirit. That's his job.

He's not going to do your praying for you. Some people think the Holy Ghost is going to do their praying for them. It's like when people say, 'God I can sit back and wait. God's got it all in control.'

That's a lie. God don't have it all in control. Somebody say, oh Brother Martin you shouldn't have said that. God only has in control what you allow him to have in control. Some people can't cast their cares upon the Lord, because when they give it to God, they take it and try to work it out. (See 1st Peter 5:7) Then God says, okay you go ahead and have it. So in that case, he doesn't have it in control.

You wonder why God don't have your attitude in control. He told YOU to humble yourself. (See James 4:10, 1 Pet 5:6) God never told you that he was going to humble you. It's not even scriptural. He said humble yourself! If you have a problem being humble the Lord will allow the enemy to come against you to help you to be humble. He'll allow the hordes of hell to come against you and then you'll be humble. Chasing you! God will allow the enemy to come against you so; you'll want to be humble. When Satan gets through bouncing you around, you'll want to be humble. You'll be so humble. You would even want to take up an offering. That's humility. That's ignorance.

How are you going to preach the gospel? We don't preach for money. Money is the farthest thing from my mind. I don't worry about it because I know what the word of God says. When I've given unto God and paid my tithes: *give and it shall be given unto me. Men will give into my bosom.* I don't have to beg people and use people to get over. My needs are met according to his riches and glory. The church is not my source. These revivals and meetings are not my source. I'm living! I'm standing on the word of God. I'm standing on the promise of God. It wouldn't make me a never mind if nobody comes up here and gets an offering envelope. God's still going to meet my needs. My

67

needs are still met according to his riches and glory because I'm a faith man and God's a faith God! (cf. Phil. 4:19)

SPIRITUAL WATCHMEN

We are talking about Intercessory prayer and we just looked at Romans 8:26. We believe in studying the word of God so when you come to these services you have to bring your Bible. Somebody say it's not that much revival in the world. But, I could go another two weeks. It wouldn't make me a never mind. I just love the word of God. I love ministering the word. I love it! I believe if God is giving you something, you ought to be faithful enough to share it. And not boast and brag about what you have except you are sharing it. We're talking about the prayer of Intercession. Isaiah 62:1-2, 6 says:

> 'For Zion's sake will I not hold my peace, and for Jerusalem's sake I will not rest (Now this is an Intercessor) until the righteousness thereof go forth as brightness, and the salvation thereof as a lamp that burneth. And the Gentiles shall see thy righteousness, and all kings thy glory: and thou shalt be called by a new name, which the mouth of the LORD shall name. I have set watchmen upon thy walls, O Jerusalem, which shall never hold their peace day nor night: ye that make mention of the LORD, keep not silence'

God says these watchmen are Intercessors! I'm going to read it in the Living Bible to show you that these watchmen that God is talking about are Intercessors. God told Ezekiel in the 33rd chapter: son of man I've made you a watchman. I've made you an Intercessor. That's why God said in Ezekiel 22:30 'I sought for a man among them to stand in the gap to make up the hedge for the land that I should not destroy it, but I found none!' God did it in Abraham's day in Sodom and Gomorrah for their sin was grievous. It grieved God because of the people's sin. *Abraham stood in the gap when God got ready to destroy Sodom and Gomorrah for their sin. (cf. Gen. 18)*

Isaiah 62:6 in the Living Bible says 'oh Jerusalem I have set Intercessors, Watchmen' Intercessors! Watchmen! Intercessors! Watchmen! Intercessors! Watchmen! 'Oh Jerusalem I have set Intercessors on your wall who shall cry to God all day and all night for the fulfillment of his promises!' Thank God for Intercessors who cry to God all day and all night for the fulfillment of his promises! God give us more Intercessors—people who will cry out all day and all night saying, God fulfill your promises! Fulfill your promises! Give us more Intercessors!

We've got more people feasting that they are fasting. We've got more people playing than they are praying. God's looking for Intercessors who will be watchmen. We are living in days and times were people—if you don't know your God you are going to be weak. Daniel 11:32 says 'those who know their God shall be strong and do exploits.' They that know their God shall be strong! Everyday I'm being strengthened by the power of his might. Zechariah 4:6 says 'this is the word of the LORD unto Zerubbabel, saying, Not by might, nor by power, but by my spirit, saith the LORD of hosts.' It's not by the power and might of an army but it's by his Holy Spirit that the work get's done.

I like the phrase that says: the word of the Lord came unto Jeremiah saying. The word of the Lord came unto Ezekiel saying. God spoke a word to me and I said it like this: The word of the Lord came unto Brother Martin saying: Son you're going to see my glory in your dwelling and in your midst. I will cause men and women to bless you and help you do what I've placed in your heart to do for me. Please be patient son. Go on doing what I've called you to do and you shall see my glory in your midst. He said I am promoting you. He said, you've been faithful in that which was least (when God say you have been faithful, you've been faithful) He said I'm going to make you faithful in that which is much. He said you've been criticized. You've been talked bad about but in the midst of it all I'm going to raise you up said the Lord.

That was back on June 29th 1987 that God spoke that word to me at 5:42 a.m. to 5:51 a.m. The Spirit of God came on me for nine minutes! I couldn't sleep. The power of God was on me so strong—God said son I want to talk to you. I want you to write. I got a pen and immediately began to write. Look! I've typed it all out and wrote it down.

> Isaiah 61:1 'The Spirit of the Lord GOD is upon me; because the LORD hath anointed me to preach good tidings unto the meek; he hath sent me to bind up the brokenhearted, to proclaim liberty to the captives, and the opening of the prison to them that are bound'

Everything on this paper, within nine minutes, I wrote it all down. And I don't take shorthand. I just obeyed the Holy Ghost. I said God you repeat it real slow and I'll write it down. The things that God does (that's why the Bible says one day with the Lord is as a thousand years.) God is awesome! Faster than a locomotive! Faster than the speed of light!

CRYING OUT TO GOD!

We're talking about Intercessory prayer here—the prayer of intercession: Isaiah chapter 62: 6-7:

I have set watchmen upon thy walls, O Jerusalem, which shall never hold their peace day nor night: ye that make mention of the LORD, keep not silence, And give him no rest, till he establish, and till he make Jerusalem a praise in the earth.

When you are praying give God no rest. See! Some of us get restless. All this week, I've been seeing people going to sleep. They come to church. They come in here and they go to sleep. They get restless. People don't want what God have. You got to love God enough to stay awake. God said he's looking for watchman, not people to come to church and snore. Wake up in Jesus name! They'll sit on the front row and sleep. They come to church to get away from it all. I guess it's the only place you can find peace.

God said in Isaiah 62:6 'Oh Jerusalem I have set Intercessors on your wall who shall cry all day and all night' (They are not sleeping! They are crying!) What do you mean crying? They're praying! You got people instead of coming to prayer meeting, they come to sleep meeting. They come to meet with God on their knees to go to sleep. You can't get anything from God. Jacob had to wrestle all night long. Wrestling denotes strenuous effort. You're releasing some energy when you're struggling. That's how he got his name changed from Jacob which means supplanter to Israel which means he struggles with God.

Now these people were crying out to God. Intercessors are crying out to God. Everyday I go to that church on 17th in Miami.

71

Everyday at 12 o'clock I meet God there. I'm crying out to God all day there. I'm swarmed up in prayer. My life is revolutionized. I'll never be the same. God is working something out in me and through me through the person and the power of the Holy Ghost and I have no glory in myself but I glory in the Lord Jesus Christ and the power of God and what God will do when people will be willing to pay the price and be persistent and be diligent and persevere about the things of God!

Some of us are slothful. You can't inherit the promise of God. God said in Hebrews 6:12 'be not slothful but be followers of them who through faith and patience inherit the promises.' You got to persevere. You got to be persistent. You got to know what it is to intercede in the spirit of God. To pull down strongholds! Some of you have little knowledge of what it is to pray in tongues, but I pray in the spirit.

God said in John 4:24, Jesus spoke these words, he said, God is a Spirit: and they that worship him' (What?) 'in spirit and in truth!' How do you worship God in the Spirit? You worship him in tongues. How do you worship God in truth? You worship him in the word. The word is the Truth!

To be honest with you the revival is just getting started in the realm of the spirit. But in the flesh, in the natural, it might be ending. But God's giving some people something to walk away with because he is pouring it out of me. He's pouring it in me and through me from heaven, and I'm receiving it. I'm eating it up so I can give it to his people. God don't give you anything for you to hold it to yourself—to walk around with a big shoulder thinking you better than anybody else. He gives it to you for you to give it away. But you can't give people something if you don't have anything. Nothing from nothing leaves nothing!

HEAVEN'S WISDOM

That's why we need to fast and pray and turn our plates down. God will give us heavenly wisdom. If we'll fast and pray and turn our plates down and get out of the flesh and get out of the carnal realm and get into the spirit. We can get something from heaven. That's why I'm not playing church. I refuse to hang out around anybody who's not serious with God. They don't mean business with God. We have nothing in common. With me, it's God or nothing! I'm not playing church! I mean business with God. If God don't mean business with me, let him leave me alone. I'll go get a job and go to work. Forget it! I don't want to waste my time.

I didn't give my life, nine years ago to come to live like the devil! To become a hypocrite! To come and do my own thing! I didn't come over here just to live defeated! To talk about what we don't have. (The wish I had. Try to get. Want to be like.) I can go out there and serve the devil the way I was and go to hell—I mean go to hell in style.

But I came over here because I know Jesus is a lover of his people. He is a Blesser! But I'm not going to hell. That's why I came over here to serve God. I didn't come over here to use God's people, to manipulate to get my needs met, to think I'm something. I want to see God's people blessed. If God prospers and blesses me you better believe I want to see you blessed and prosperous. If I'm blessed to drive a fine car, you better believe I want to see you driving a fine car. If I'm blessed with the nicer things in life, I don't want it all for myself. You better believe I want to see you blessed. You got some people that are selfish in this way. They want the whole hog.

CALLED TO BE HOLY

An Intercessor is one who stands in the gap like Abraham did for Sodom and Gomorrah. That city was wicked. The men wanted to go to bed and have a relationship with the angels. That's how wicked it was. We find that same spirit of homosexuality running rampant throughout today. We find the spirit of harlotry running rampant throughout today. Drug addiction! Alcoholism! You got God's people dib dabbing in sin. We got to get the sin out church! We got to straighten from the pulpit to the door. We got to clean our lives up! We got to clean our lives up! We are living in a day and time in this generation that God is calling for holiness. He's calling for us to live a righteous life. You got people who say Brother Martin, I can't live holy.

You're a liar. You don't want to live holy. You can live holy. If you say you can't live holy, you're calling God a liar because he said *be ye holy as I am holy.* You're saying God is not holy. He can't live holy. That's what you're saying, when you say you can't live holy. Paul said 'I can do all things though Christ which strengthen me.'(Phil. 4:13) If you can get out there and live like the devil then you can live for God. You got people who it is very easy for them to live for the devil. Some people are to the place and the point where they have made their minds up to live for the devil.

WATCHMAN ON THE WALL

People tell me it takes a well made up mind to serve God. It takes a Christ like mind to serve God. Phil. 2:5 said 'let this mind be in you which is also in Christ Jesus.' The Bible didn't say a well made up mind. The Bible said have the mind of Christ or the attitude of Christ. Some things that we say and that we speak are not in the Bible.

Some little clichés we use they are not in the word of God. There is no scriptural reference for it. I have heard some people say that God said 'if you take one step, I'll take two.' That's a lie. That's not in the Bible. That's something you said. There's no chapter and verse in that. 'Charity starts at home and spreads abroad.' That's a good saying but it's not in the Bible. It's not biblical. It's not scripture. Charity does start at home and spreads abroad but it's not in the Bible. We've taken some things we have said that's not in the Bible and put chapter and verse to them and we've deceived ourselves to hell! We're confused! We've got a lot of religious stuff and God's sick of it. Tradition! I don't say anything that the Bible doesn't say because it's a lie. That's why God said 'let every man be a liar and let God be true.' (Romans 3:4)

If you're standing behind the pulpit teaching and preaching, and you can't give me chapter and verse, I'm not going to listen to you. And I'm humble too. I don't have to disrespect you and your meeting. I'm just going to get up and politely walk out. For, I refuse to listen to that. You're not feeding my spirit.

Then you got people, they want to sing all the time in church but they don't have any word in them. They have no knowledge of casting out devils. Just like that girl, that sister we had to set her free—expel some unclean spirits. I'm used to that. I'm used to casting out devils.

75

It's not too much that gone on in church that I'm not acquainted with. I've been preaching for nine years. I've never had a devil or anybody to come in any meeting that I am in to tell me that I didn't have the power of God to cast him out. Not one—because I know where I stand with God! The devil knows that I mean business. I'm not playing with the devil. Just like Jesus said *I beheld Satan as fallen from heaven as lighting*—I'll cast the devil out! Jesus said 'if I cast out devils with the Finger of God then you know the Kingdom of God has come unto you.' (cf. Luke 11:20)

When you stand on the word of God and you know where you stand in God's word, no devil in hell or from hell can stop you! Because the word of God will draw the fine line! Playing church days are over. The one man show is over. You got people, they are all for self. My ministry! They say. What about the ministry of Jesus? Jesus wants to raise the dead. He told me that last night. I was going to bed and he said son I want to raise the dead. I said Lord whatever you want to do, you go ahead and do it. It's fine with me. I have no problems with that. Jesus wants to heal the sick. There are some people that are sin sick. They got a disease. They just can't live for God. I want you to know God loves you and he can heal you from that. Jesus is the Great Physician.

He said I come not to call the righteous but sinners to repentance. If you are in here tonight and you don't know Christ is your Lord and Savior, you are lost. That's the whole purpose of this meeting to see you come to God. God doesn't want anybody to go to hell. One thing I found out about the truth, you can't compromise.

WATCH AND PRAY

You can't compromise the word of God. You're going to find people sleeping and slumbering and the enemy is going to come in and take their life in church. Why? Because they are not watching! Jesus disciples went to sleep. They weren't watchful. (Cf. Mt. 26:40-41)

I came in the church today and I saw something. I sneaked in. I could have come in there and killed everybody that was in there. They all had their backs turned. If I was a thief I could have grabbed the women pocketbooks and stole everything they had in there. I could've killed them all. Blew their brains out! Stabbed them! Stuck them in the head! They were all in their praying. Everybody inside and the door was open and I snuck in. Nobody even knew I was in there. Church people are ignorant. Jesus said not just pray, but WATCH as well as pray. You tell me to close my eyes. I might close one of them but I'm going to look to see what you're doing. I'm going to watch and pray.

Unsaved people think that Christian people are really kind of awkward because we do some backward things. We get so saved until we loose all of our common sense. You got to watch people now. While you are sitting in church and got your eyes closed a brother will be going in your purse. When you get back home you'll say I know that I had fifty dollars in my purse. I'm telling you things that have happened to people. It has already happened and is happening.

If I leave my Bible in church, you will be surprised who will walk out with it even though it's got my name and address on it in big print. Would they return it? No. They will say they found it when it's got my name and address on it. You took it. You stole it. It was in the church. You should have left it where you saw it at. Not too many people will say amen on that but it's still so anyhow. It's getting kind of hot in here. I'm talking about word hot. I'm making some true statements. Some of the clichés we say, we use, that's all good but they're not biblical. They're not scriptural. There are not based on what the word of God teaches. They are good and they're prophetic but we can't take them for chapter and verse.

I hear people say that 'God is a mystery.' He may be a mystery to you but he is not a mystery to me because I have the spirit of revelation. God is not a mystery. He's a mystery to you if you don't have the Holy Spirit. The Spirit of God will reveal God to you. The Bible says 'the secret things belong to the Lord.' (Deut. 29:29) Now if I got him living on the inside of me. Didn't he say 'the Holy Spirit will reveal all things to you and bring back all things to your remembrance' (John. 14:26) He's the Spirit of Truth. The Holy Ghost is the Spirit of Truth. (cf. 1 John. 5:6)

God don't leave his people dumb and ignorant. I don't know about you but I'm not ignorant. I consider myself intelligent because God's intelligent. God's not ignorant. God is not going around saying, 'How did that light come into being?'

As a man of God, I have said a lot of things but I can't apologize for the truth. One thing for sure and Pastor Bullard knows this and that is I'm dedicated to the work of God. But God deals with me so strong that sometimes, I don't even understand myself. He's shaking me! My life is being shaken in that prayer closet. After being in the presence of Jesus, you will never be the same!

1. What is an Intercessor? Discuss the qualifications.

2. According to Romans 8:2-27 how does the Holy Spirit support with prayers?

3. If we don't cast our care upon the Lord as described in 1st Peter 2:7 is that evidenced that we are in control and trying to handle it?

4. What does it mean to be humble?

5. If God is in control of our lives according to Phil. 4:19 what will He do?

6. According to Isaiah 62:1-2, 6 what does a watchman do?

7. Discuss a Watchman-Intercessor in relation to Ezekiel 22:30?

8. How did Abraham in Genesis 18 exemplify traits of an intercessor?

9. If you don't know God you are going to be weak. What does Daniel 11:32 say about strength?

10. Zechariah 4:6 says it's not by _____ nor by _____ but by His Holy Spirit.

11. Isaiah 61:1 says what about the Spirit of the Lord?

12. When God calls us to prayer, does He call us to a sleep meeting?

13. You can't inherit the promises of God if you are slothful. What does Hebrews 6:12 say?

14. You got to persevere and be persistent in prayer to bring down
_____.

15. According to John 4:24, how must we worship God?

16. We can incorporate _____ and praying for heavenly wisdom.

17. Once you are saved, are you called to be holy? Can you live holy?

18. It takes a Christ-like mind to serve God. What does Philippians 2:5 reveal?

19. How are common clichés that we use different from the word of God? (pp. 80, 81)

20. What did Jesus say about casting out demons in Luke 11:20?

21. Deut. 29:29 says 'the _____ things belong to the Lord.' A person can be sin sick. A person can also compromise the truth. Where do you stand with God?

23. What did Jesus say in Matthew 26:40-41 about praying and being watchful?

26. The Holy Ghost is the Spirit of _____. What does John 26 say about the Holy Spirit?

PART II

THE VISION

"Wait a minute! There is some FOG in this building. The glory of God is in this building. I see it!"

3.2

We didn't come to this meeting tonight to lift up the devil but we came to lift up Jesus. We came to let Trinity Christian Fellowship know that Jesus Christ is still performing miracles. We came to let you know that our hearts are encouraged in the Lord. I'm going to talk about the power of prayer, what prayer will do when you find people praying and getting serious with God–meaning business with God. That's why the devil's mad. He can't stop us.

I was at the church today at 12 o'clock in Intercessory prayer at the Outreach of Excitement where Mother Ruth is the Pastor, praising God and worshipping Jesus. Not too many people showed up there and some people were discouraged. I said to the people that showed up: you come here to pray, didn't you? Let's pray. Let's get down to business with God. I said anything you want from God you can get it right now at the altar. You don't need me or anybody else to lay there hands on you. Whatever you want from God you can get on your knees and get it. (See Matt. 18:19) Some people are looking for some confirmation or some laying on of hands of some man. God wants to give you what he wants you to have He's the only one that can give it to you. God has what you need.

Father God in Jesus name, I ask you to bless your people Lord. Give them a listening ear and a receptive heart to receive the word of God. Sir we do want to honor you, to give you the glory, to give you the praise. Satan we bind you. We take authority over you in Jesus name. We command you to go! Loose God's people! I command you devil. I break your power Satan! Enough is enough! Now you get out of here and go now! In Jesus name! Enough is enough, devil! And God we give you the praise in Jesus name.

I've had all I'm going to take off of the devil tonight. The devil knows how to get you. If he can get you upset, he knows God can't use you. If he can get you mad with the people, mad because somebody came late. People didn't show up on time and then they want to sing all night and stop you from ministering. I have to obey the Lord.

Sometimes folks want to sing all night but you can't sing over the word. Jesus said 'heaven and earth shall pass away but my word will last forever.' (Mt. 24:35) People need the word of God. We can sing one song but let's get into the word or let's get into prayer. Some things that we prolong the time with in God's house, we need to cut them aside and cut them down. But don't cut the word because the word of God will save your life. The word of God will heal people.

The word of God will bring people out. I watched a man yesterday come up to the altar because we been in that church praying. He came up to the altar convicted of sin. Nobody laid hands on him. Nobody touched him and devils were coming out of his body because of Intercessory prayer because people came to meet with God. We need to meet with God.

We need to come to a place and a point where we are willing to spend time with God on our face. The devil's been doing everything he can to discourage the people of God as a people. You saw what happened tonight all of the little odds and ends, the confusion and the mess. I told Elder Peterson, I said I'm going to keep my cool tonight. I'm going to show the devil who he is dealing with. I'm a man of God! Ain't no devil in hell going to cause me too loose my cool. I'm mad with the devil. I'm getting the real enemy. You're not my enemy. The devil is.

Sometimes we think that we are one another's enemies but the devil is your real enemy. Anytime you are having a problem, it's the devil at work! Take that devil! Messing around with the equipment and messing around with everything. Trying to get me to loose my cool, but I got the victory over you devil.

I know that we've all been going but God's doing a great work. What the enemy wants us to do is get us discouraged. Get us tired, worn out and weak, where we can't do anything for God. We loose the vision. He'll break up marriages if he can do it. If you let him do it, Satan will destroy lives and homes.

He'll have the pastor like he standing alone. He'll have the people on one side and the pastor on the other side so he can come in and split the church down the middle. Jesus said anytime a house is divided… That goes for a church house. That goes for a home. That goes for any kind of organization, any business enterprise—a house divided against itself, it shall not—it can not stand!

You got to be unified. You got to become one. The spirit of God is not going to enter into a place where there is strife, division and confusion. People are jealous of one another. They won't love one another. Psalms 133:1 says 'how good and pleasant it is for brethren to dwell together in unity.' I preached a message titled, "Together we stand." Wait a minute! There is some FOG in this building. The glory of God is in this building. I see it!

GOD WANTS TO MEET WITH YOU

We're talking about the power of prayer tonight and tonight church we are going to pray. We are going to get out of the flesh and get into the spirit. We are going to make contact with God tonight. We are going to touch God. God said call my people back to prayer. Call them back to their knees. We need to go back to the altar and cry God spare thy people! It's not time to play. It's time to pray. It's time to spend time with God. It's time to get on our face before God. It's time to meet with God. Like God told Moses to bring out his people. God said Moses bring my people out so I can meet with them. God wants to meet with you. I'll show you in Exodus 19:7-8: 'And Moses came and called for the elders of the people, and laid before their faces all these words which the LORD commanded him. And all the people answered together, and said, All that the LORD hath spoken we will do.'

How does God speak? God has a voice. God speaks by his word. God is speaking in this place tonight. But I wander if we can hear his voice? God is in this place tonight. I see a literal cloud in this building. That's why the devil's been fighting tonight. That's why the devils been trying to get me upset because the power of God—God is going to manifest himself tonight. I don't have to touch you. The glory of God is in this place. That's why the devil's been fighting tonight. This place is clouded up with the glory of God. I can see it! I don't have to touch you. God wants to meet with you.

If you are in the church and you are not living the way God wants you to live you might die in the presence of Almighty God because that glory—you won't be able to stand his presence because of the glory. You better make sure you are living right. That glory is coming into manifestation. When the priest went into the Holy of Holies, (where God's power was shut up in, where that Shekinah Glory came in) if they were not living right, they died when they went in there. They died!

That goes for the pulpit too. God's going to sanctify the altar. And people that are not walking right, preachers and ministers that stand behind that sacred desk, and their lives are not clean according to the word of God, they are going to die. God told me, he said they are going to die son. They are going to die! And if you are one of them and you are not living right, you are going to die too!

The glory of God is in manifestation. God wants to meet with his people. Playing church days are over. That's why the devil's mad and he is upset. You watched tonight as he did everything he could in the natural to make me upset to make me loose my cool so I wouldn't have the anointing to minister to you. You loose that anointing when you loose your cool—getting in the flesh about it. I refuse to get in the flesh. I'm going to stay in the spirit. If you stay in the spirit you'll be sweet even when the devil's coming up against you and attacking you. You'll stay sweet. You'll keep your cool.

> 'And the LORD said unto Moses, Lo, I come unto thee in a thick cloud, that the people may hear when I speak with thee, and believe thee for ever. And Moses told the words of the people unto the LORD. And the LORD said unto Moses, Go unto the people, and sanctify them to day and to morrow, and let them wash their clothes,' (Exodus 19: 9-10)

I told you that I saw a cloud in this building tonight. God's saying, wash your clothes! God's saying he wants you to be sanctified. What do you mean? He wants to set you apart. God's calling for people to live holy. He's calling for people to live righteous! That's why the devils mad. I see the glory of God in this place. I see a literal cloud.

WASH YOUR CLOTHES!

> Verse 10 'And the LORD said unto Moses, Go unto the people, and sanctify them to day and to morrow, and let them wash their clothes.'

I'm coming unto you tonight, like God said, go unto the people and sanctify them. (He didn't say tomorrow first) He said today and tomorrow. God wants you to live holy tonight, tomorrow and next week, next month and next year until the day you leave here. This is a strong message. That's why the devil was fighting this word. But it's going to cause people to be blessed and to come into closeness with God.

I can't get your attention, to attract your attention to me. God said son point my people to me. If any man love God and love God's people, he is going to point people to God. He is going to say what God says. Because if he says God's talking to him, then God's going to tell him like Moses, bring my people unto me Moses. I want to meet with them. I want to talk to my people. Moses didn't lift his self up like a god but God said Moses I'm going to send you like a god. You are going to be a ruler and a deliverer. Why? Because the spirit of God was upon Moses to lead God's people in his time, yet, the people were rebellious. They took Moses through some things. Moses went through a lot with those rebellious people.

> Exodus 19:11-12 'And be ready against the third day: for the third day the LORD will come down in the sight of all the people upon Mount Sinai. And thou shalt set bounds unto the people round about, saying, Take heed to yourselves, that ye go not up into the mount, or touch the border of it: whosoever toucheth the mount shall be surely put to death'

God said if you touch that place, you touch that altar and you're not living right your going to die. Sin cannot stand in the presence of God. God said it stinks in my nostrils. 'The wages of sin is death (Romans 6:23) but the gift of God' (What gift of God?) The Holy Ghost! The Spirit of God is the gift of God. He is eternal life. We've had the dispensation of God the Father. We've had the dispensation of the Son. God the Father is the creative word. Jesus is the living word and the Holy Spirit is the Eternal Word. You can read it in Hebrews 9:14. We're living in the dispensation of the spirit of God. This is the last move. We've had the former rain and this is the latter rain. We are the generation that's experiencing this latter rain.

> 'There shall not an hand touch it, but he shall surely be stoned, or shot through; whether it be beast or man, it shall not live: when the trumpet sound long, they shall come up to the mount. And Moses went down from the mount unto the people, and sanctified the people; and they washed their clothes. And he said unto the people, be ready against the third day: come not at your wives.' (Exodus 19:13-15)

Do you know why? You have no business having no relationship with your wife when you are before God. You might destroy yourself trying to do such a thing. 1st Corinthians the 7th chapter is about husbands and wives. When you want something from God and you're seeking God, you're fasting and praying—you have no business having a sexual relationship. God said abstain from that. God wants to meet with you. God wants us to live clean lives. God wants us to live holy lives. God wants us to sanctify ourselves that we might receive of God. The only person I am loving and having an intimate relationship with is Jesus, not any flesh. God wants you be intimate with him. It's like a man and a woman having intercourse. God wants you to be intimate with him.

> 'And it came to pass on the third day in the morning, that there were thunders and lightings, and a thick cloud upon

the mount, and the voice of the trumpet exceeding loud;
so that all the people that was in the camp trembled.'
(Exodus 19:16)

When God starts talking, people are going to tremble. The people said to Moses: Moses, we don't want to hear a thing you got to say—shut up! We'll hear what Gods got to say. God started speaking like thundering and lighting. Then the people said, God stop talking. God you are hurting our ears. We will hear what Moses has to say. God said shut up and listen to him then!

You got people who say we don't want to hear the pastor, we want to hear God. When you hear God (and you're in disobedience) you're going to be on the wrong side of him. God gave you a pastor to feed you with knowledge and understanding. Jeremiah 3:15 says 'And I will give you pastors according to mine heart.' That's why we need to study to show ourselves approved unto God. I'm not playing church. I'm not playing ministry. I'm not playing preaching.

I'm studying, I'm praying, I'm seeking the face of God. I refuse to stand up before an audience of people and not have it together with God. I'm not trying to impress you. You don't have anything you can give me or you can offer me. You can't buy me. I am not for sale. I refuse to compromise. I'm going to make sure, I'm living what I'm preaching out of that book because the word comes to me first.

GOD'S CLEANING HOUSE

Judgment shall begin at the house of God. And it's going to start from the pulpit to the door! He said, sanctify your selves! Purify yourselves! Wash your clothes! Clean your life up. Be ye holy for it is written I am holy. (cf. 1Peter 4:17, James 4:8, Leviticus 20:7)

You got some people that say I can't live holy. That's a lie. Sister Steele said people come to her and tell her that they can't live holy. She tells them that they are a liar. They can live holy. Your flesh doesn't want to live holy. You got to pray and fast and put the flesh under. That's what's wrong with us. We're so fleshly and naturally inclined that we can't receive anything from the spirit.

That's why God told me, he didn't want me hanging around certain people. They are saved. They are born again but he doesn't want me staying with them or living with them. I'm ready to get out of there so I can spend time with God instead of being around people with spirits in them fighting you. There are spirits in the people fighting you because they're Christians but they don't want to live close to God. They're going half the way. The devil's going to knock you down! It's all or nothing with God.

God's calling people to sanctification. He is calling men and women of God to get their eyes off of self and their own little tidbit ministry and get their eyes on Christ and point people to Jesus. Point people to God! Tell people God is the answer to their problem. People want you to counsel them all night. Come on let's counsel.

Let's go to the Father. He's the counselor of all. Let's get on this altar. I'm going to counsel you alright. We're going to talk to God and when you get up, you're going to get the answer. You're going to have the answer to your prayer because you're going to pray. I'm not going to do it for you.

You just want me to lay hands on you and give you a little quick fix so you can go back out and do your own thing. It's not going to happen like that. You're going to have to live holy. You've got to live right!

People are sick because their tipping and sipping. They got some little secret sin. I remember Brother Jimmy Swaggert preached a message about 'That Thing.' I wonder if he knew what he was talking about. He preached a message about 'That Thing'. What is that thing in your life? I'm trying to find that thing in mine. Before I take the mote out of somebody else eye, I'm going to take the beam out of mine— before I try to judge somebody else. I don't want to be a hypocrite. Preachers love to stand behind the pulpit and just *yaw* at people. They know they're not living anything themselves. That thing hit the wall and come back at me because I'm talking about preachers now. That's why we need to get on our knees and pray!

(****)

People are getting blessed and people are getting encouraged and lifted. And the people that need to be here are not here. God wants to meet with his people. Exodus 19:17 'And Moses brought forth the people out of the camp to meet with God; and they stood at the nether part of the mount.' How many preachers? How many ministers? How many leaders have brought God's people out to meet with him? That's what this teaching (not preaching) is all about to bring people out to meet with God. If you don't want anything from God then don't show up. If you're not real and you're playing church don't come here because all this week I'm going to teach on prayer—the power of prayer.

We're going to intercede. We're going to pray. The greatest meeting that's happening inside the church (that makes the church) is prayer, and you find people don't show up. You got folks that don't want to pray. They want to eat. If I tell all of you people to fast with me so many hours a day during this week of revival, you couldn't do it. Your flesh won't let you. You say, 'I got to work. I work all night.' So what? I work all night too. Sometimes twenty-four hours I pray. I'm praying for you while you're in the bed sleep. I can't sleep. God's telling me to get up and pray for people. He tells me to pray for these leader's that are falling—these men of God that's falling into sin. I'm sowing a seed so I don't fall because I can fall.

MATTERS OF THE HEART

Verse 17 'And Moses brought forth the people out of the camp to meet with God....'

You got to come out of your own little camp. Your own little attitude! Your own little ways about this thing! Come out of that mess! God wants to meet with you. But he is not going to meet with you under your conditions. He's going to meet with you according to his word by his Spirit. He is going to deal with your heart. But you say listen Brother Martin, I got this thing in my life. I know that. God knows that too but he wants to deal with it. He wants to help you overcome that thing.

It might be a cigarette habit. It might be a drug habit. It might be an attitude. It might be you always putting people down. You're always getting upset all the time. You're always getting mad and fidgety about everything. God wants to help you deal with it. He wants to help you to overcome that thing. God don't want you bound! I don't care what kind of habits you have. God wants to liberate you. He wants to meet with you so he can help you.

You say Brother Martin but I'm wrestling. I'm wrestling with this thing. You need to pray and fast and lock in with God until God give you the victory in your spirit. Paul said I die (not two days a week) but he said, 'I die daily!' (1 Cor. 15:31) You got to put the flesh under everyday of your life. You should fast so many hours out of the day. I do—to put the flesh under. So I know when I'm walking in the flesh. Tonight if I had gotten into the flesh you would have known about it. The devil's not going to make a mess out of me. I showed the devil something. I kept my cool. I stood right at that door and I told Elder Peterson that Satan did everything he could.

He tried to bring thoughts to my mind. I blocked them—the thoughts that the devil brought to my mind about the people being late. I said I don't want that junk. You can keep that Satan. I don't want that mess. Keep it! It's time for us to straighten up and get our act together as ministers of God. We need to treat people right. I love God but I say God I love your people. I refuse to wound, beat up and hurt God's people. (See Rev. 3:19)

Sometimes God through his word will chasten his people. God will chasten his people, not me but God. The word will do it. And I'm going to make sure my spirit is right when I'm giving the word. I'm going to make sure I'm right because the word that I'm preaching is going to judge me.

> Verse 18 'And Mount Sinai was altogether on a smoke, because the LORD descended upon it in fire' Why? Because when God shows up it's awesome! 'And the smoke thereof ascended as the smoke of a furnace, and the whole mount quaked greatly.' Why? Because God was standing there!

> Verse 19 'and when the voice of the trumpet sounded long, and waxed louder and louder, Moses spake, and God answered him by a voice.'

God answered him by a—what? Not a word. God answered him by a voice. *God's looking for Intercessors to stand in the gap and make up the hedge on behalf of His people!*

1. According to Matthew 18:18-19 two or three people can do what in prayer?

2. We need the word of God. Matthew 24:35 says that the word of God will heal people and _____ people of sin.

3. We should not cut the _____ or cut _____ prayer because it brings deliverance.

4. The enemy is not people but the real enemy is the _____.

5. In Matthew 12:25 what did Jesus say about a house divided?

6. Psalm 133:1 says how _____ and _____ it is for brethren to dwell together in _____.

7. We got to get out of the _____ and get into the spirit and make contact with God.

8. In Exodus 19 Moses was instructed to bring the people out to _____ with God.

9. God is saying to his people regarding living a holy life wash your clothes. God is _____ the altar.

10. The Glory of God will _____ in our presence when we pray.

11. The devil will do everything in the natural that he can to attempt to get you to loose your cool so that you will loose the _____.

12. Does God want you to live sanctified, holy and set apart?

13. Sin cannot stand in God's presence. Sin stinks in Hs nostrils. 'The _____ of sin is _____ but the gift of God is _____ life.' (Rom 6:23)

14. Discuss Hebrews 9:14 regarding the dispensation.

15. What does 1st Cor. 7 say about husbands and wives sexual relations when it comes to fasting and seeking God's face?

16. Pastors are given to feed us knowledge and understanding. Jeremiah 3:15 says what?

17. Judgment shall begin at the house of _____.

18. Can people as well as Christians have spirits in them that fight against you?

19. Do some Christians go half the way with God?

20. Can you be so fleshly inclined that you can't receive from the Spirit?

21. True ministers point people to God and not themselves. (True or False)

22. Do you believe that a Christian can have secret sin?

23. The greatest meeting happening that makes the church is _____ yet people don't show up.

24. Are certain forms of prayer labor and work? Explain your answer.

25. God will meet with you according to His _____ and according to His Spirit.

26. (See Rev. 3:19) With loving kindness God draws us but He will chasten those whom He loves. (True or False)

TRAVAILING PRAYER

PART I

SPIRITUAL BIRTHING

"It's praying time, not playing time. It's time to pray! You got saints feasting when they ought to be fasting. And you got saints playing when they ought to be praying. It's not time to feast! It's time to fast! It's not time to play! It's time to pray!"

4.1

This section discusses the victory of bringing some things forth in the spirit realm through the process of spiritual birthing. It is very similar to that of natural childbirth. In natural childbirth the pain is such that even modern medication may fail to relieve all of it. And the labor is actually very hard work. Bringing forth a baby is hard work. I have travailed and brought forth some things in the spirit. And that's hard work. I mean years, years have gone into this thing. That's why I'm very careful because I done seen what happened to too many and I just refuse to fall. It don't take that much to see what time it is. You say what time is it?

It's praying time, not playing time. It's time to pray! You got saints feasting when they ought to be fasting. And you got saints playing when they ought to be praying. It's not time to feast! It's time to fast! It's not time to play! It's time to pray! If you pray you will stay. If you are too slow, you're gone have to go!

This pain (Now I'm talking about a woman bringing forth a child.) This part is necessary and might be labeled the dying part of a mother's experience only as she willingly suffers. Only as this mother willingly suffers can new life come forth. Now I'm suffering for a lot of people. I have a burden on me for souls. To see men and women come into the Kingdom of God. Like on last night. This dear precious sister right here, I went home talking about that. I went home rejoicing. I went home saying, Oh Jesus that's what you called me to do. I went home weeping, breaking and crying. I went home saying oh I love you so much Jesus. It thank you Lord. I worship you Jesus. I thank you Lord for that sister's soul. Heaven was shouting last night!

I got ready to get in the bed and the power of God came on me last night. Sometimes when the power of God comes on me, I can't sleep. I say Lord if you don't take this power off of me, Lord I can't go to sleep. I'm tired and I want to rest. Sometimes, I don't even know how tired I am until I lay down. When we get there to the church at 12 o'clock and get to praying, we don't get out sometimes until about 5 o'clock. We're counseling and praying with people. Concerned— showing love and compassion.

This week will be a prayer seminar. We're teaching a long the lines of prayer—travail. Romans 8:22 says 'for we know that the whole creation groaneth and travaileth in pain together until now.' (God said the whole creation) ...until now. A human birth is almost somewhat like the birth of an animal. I've watched animal birth before and they travail. God said the whole creation. An animal is a part of God's creation. God said the whole creation groaneth.

When a person is in pain or they are suffering, they're going to groan and agonize. When a woman is going through labor she is agonizing. She might be giving breath blows. I've never seen a woman give birth but I just know that. I've watched some women when they get into Intercessory prayer and it's like they are having a baby. They make sounds of uh! Ugh! Ugh! Those groans, those breath blows. I've watched women that pray. That travail in the spirit. They are giving birth to things in the spirit realm. That's labor. That's hard work! (cf. Rev. 12:2)

That's fatigue on the body. Toil! Travail is labor. Labor means to work. Travail is to suffer with the pains of childbirth. Severe toil! The word toil defined: is to exert strength continuously with pain and fatigue of body and mind, particularly the body. It means to labor with pain. Travail is energy. Let's establish that.

Real travail concerns the energy that we put into our praying. Some people don't get anything out of prayer but I do. I get in prayer and I begin to lock in Intercessory prayer or travail and I can stop the devils work right here on the face of this earth. I can stop it!

The devil thought he could stop this sister from coming to God last night but he couldn't. I had already prayed for her. I had already gotten the victory. For everything that's going to take place in the service, I've already gotten the victory for it. That's why I don't come in here worried saying oh God what are you going to do? I know what he is going to do. I've already gotten the victory for it. I've already prayed. I don't wait until I get in the back at the church. I prayed before I left home. I prayed all the way here, riding in the back of the car. I didn't say anything to Elder Peterson and his daughter. I was quiet the whole time we were riding because I was praying. I was talking to God.

God does not hear us because of the length of our prayers but because of the sincerity of our prayers. I can get down here and pray in five minutes and talk to God in tongues and get the victory. Somebody else can get up here, scream and holler and make a bunch of fuss and racket for an hour and don't get anything. They weren't sincere about it. They don't get anything from God.

There are times, I don't believe in praying all night. I don't believe in wasting God's time or in wasting my precious time because I'm a business man. I don't half do things. I don't half-step with God and God don't half-step with me. I mean business! I'm a business man for God. I'm not playing church. I didn't come out of the world to serve God to play with him, to be a carnal Christian. To live defeated. To be overcome. To be walked over by the devil and the demons of hell.

I came over to this side to live a victorious life. I'm more than a conqueror! Some of us live like the conquered, instead of the conqueror. We live like the victims instead of the victor. God wants you to be a victor! You are a victor. You are a conqueror. Greater is he that is in thee than he that is in the world.

God said in the 1st Epistle of John 4:4 'ye are of God, little children, and have overcome them: because greater is he that is in you, than he that is in the world.' How do you know that you have overcome them? *Because greater is he* Who? The Holy Spirit of God! Some people say the Holy Ghost or the spirit of God. He is the spirit of God. He is the spirit of promise. He is the glory of God. He is the very power of God. He is the very life of God. He will help you travail.

The Apostle Paul writing to the Galatians church said in chapter 4:19 'my little children, of whom I travail in birth again until Christ be formed in you.' Paul said my little children, I'm travailing, I'm toiling! I'm laboring! Look Paul said I'm going through labor. I'm having a baby! I'm suffering birth pangs until Christ be formed in you. How did Paul do it? He put energy into his prayers until it brought fatigue to his body.

The longest I ever prayed in my life was twelve hours. I prayed in tongues. I felt like I was dead when I got through praying that long. But the glory of God, heaven filled my soul. Have you ever had the power of God come into your room and get all over you? You pray like that. You start spending time with God and getting into his presence.

People who are not where they should be with God will feel very uncomfortable around you. You know I look at some of the things that God has allowed me to go through—the tests and trials and I say the devil meant the thing for hurt, harm and evil but God turned it around for good because I love him. I love Jesus. I'm in love with Jesus!

Prayer is not to be measured by the yard or by the pound. Prayer is to be measured by the might and the force of it. Prayer is power with God! Jacob proved that. He didn't let God go. He stayed. He prevailed. He overcame! He got the victory! Prayer is communion with God. Prayer is fellowshipping with God. It's joining forces with God. Now some people want me to get up here and put on some kind of religious tantrum. However, as ministers, sometimes we need to just come down and explain some things. Teaching is explaining. Preaching is proclaiming. And we need to have some things explained. Some people want me to jump around and shout. I'm not your everyday emotional preacher.

MATURE SONS OF GOD

I'm spending time in the presence of God. I'm growing up. I read 1st Corinthians chapter thirteen every night before I go to bed and when I get up in the morning. I don't read anything else. I've been doing it so long until Jesus is just blessing me with his love. Now a particular verse of scripture in 1st Corinthians chapter 13 caught me. I looked at it. That thing blew me! I've been reading this passage so long but I said wait a minute: Paul said 'when I was a child, I spake as a child when I became a man I put away childish things.' (1 Cor. 13:11) I said I'm no longer a child Lord. Paul said when I was a child—God was letting me know that some of his people haven't grown up yet because they are still talking like children. We are all his children but he wants us to mature and grow up. Paul said when I was a child I spoke as a child. Then I became a man. He said when he was a child and used to play with childish things he put them away. He even put away the way he talked like a child.

Some of us adults don't act like adults. Some of us that are spiritual we don't really come to the place and the point where we allow the word of God to rule and govern our lives. We have a spiritual outlook but God wants to do something inwardly in our inward man. Paul said the outward man decayeth but the inward man is renewed day by day because the word of God is prevailing.

And when the word of God is prevailing in your life, and you're travailing in prayer, you are going to die! Now I've died. I died to a lot of things. I died to television. I let television go in my life. I turned the dumb thing off. I don't watch television. I'm immune to it. I can go anywhere and shut up in a room with God twenty-four hours and I don't have to see anybody. I don't have to drink water. I can spend time with God. I know what it's like when you're in the presence of God. You don't need any water when you're in God's presence. I went all day without water. I didn't drink a drop. I was in the presence of Jesus, loving him, fellowshipping with him and loving my Father.

ETERNAL CONSECRATION

When you live your life consecrated and dedicated to God, people don't understand you. You got some people that walk half the way with God—part of the way. And I want to reach out to them but I said God I don't want to loose what you gave me because some people want you to touch them but they don't really want to touch Jesus. If you don't want to reach out and touch Jesus, then I can't help you because if you put your eyes on me and not him you're going to be disappointed. That's what has happened to a lot of people. They put their eyes on a leader. They put their eyes on an Evangelist and when he fall (when he has fallen) their God has fallen. Then they are deceived and they end up back in the world.

You got a lot of people who don't want to come to God because of what's happening in Christendom today, church stuff. There's a great falling away. We need to travail. There is a great falling away among God's people. The husband want to go this way and the wife want to go that way. But I made up my mind that I was going to walk with God whether my wife walk out on me or not. I said Jesus I'm going to walk with you if I have to walk alone. I see myself now. I see I got to walk alone. I got to walk with Jesus. I got to love him.

MARRIAGE IS COVENANT

For those of you that are married, the Bible says in Matthew 19 verse 6 'what God has joined together let no man put asunder.' You have no business leaving your husband or your wife. You are blessed. You have no business going your own way and doing your own thing. If you're having a problem in your relationship, you need to pray about it. You need to take it to God in prayer. Say to your spouse, honey let's pray!

I wish I could stop right here and take a side journey and just tell you some things about myself but it wouldn't bear repeating it. The testimony is glory to the devil. And one thing I don't do is stand behind God's podium to glorify the devil! He's not worth the testimony. And I don't have any after affect of anything I've gone through because I love Jesus.

And to love Jesus you got to love everybody. I don't care what they did to you. I don't care what they said. You got to forgive. The Bible says in Ephesians 4:32 'and be ye kind one to another, tenderhearted, forgiving one another, even as God for Christ's sake hath forgiven you.' So you have to forgive. If you are holding onto a spirit somebody done said something and did something to you, you need to forgive. You need to let it go. Save it. Don't hold on to it. Let it go!

You can't see that the devil is deceiving you. You can't see that Satan is blinding you to do something that's going to cause you pain and hurt. I am acquainted with pain. I am acquainted with hurt. I know hurt. I know what it is to hurt! I've been hurt! I know what it is when you give your heart and love somebody and they take your love and stomp on it. I know what it is when you love somebody and give your heart and you come back and somebody took the one that you love. Don't tell me hurt because I've been there.

I know what I'm talking about. I got a testimony. If I could take the side journey but the Lord say's son, don't glorify the devil. I've already gotten victory over that. It's been years. I know what it is. That's why I encourage married people to stay married. Love your spouse. Love your husband. Love your wife. God said it in his word: 'Husbands love your wives. Wives submit to your husbands.' If he's not saved, you obey the word of God. Your chaste conversation will win him. (cf. Ephesians 5)

Some of you are saved both husband and wife but you can't get along. Why is that, because somebody doesn't want to submit. Somebody don't want to acknowledge that their wrong. Somebody don't want to admit that their having a problem, that the devil is coming against them. We need to acknowledge these things and consider these things and let's pray. We can change some things if we pray. That's what's wrong with us, we are talking too much. We're looking at what the devil is doing. You got to be careful what you say.

POWER OF THE TONGUE

The moment you let the word divorce come out of your mouth, you're going to have what you say. You better keep that word out of your home. You better keep that word out of your mouth. You better keep that word out of your relationship and out of your marriage because it will come to pass. The Bible says in Proverbs 18:21 'that death and life are in the power of the tongue and they that loveth it shall eat the fruit thereof.' You better be careful what you say. Jesus said in Mark 11:23 'that whosoever shall say unto this mountain, Be thou removed, and be thou cast into the sea; and shall not doubt in his heart, but shall believe that those things which he saith shall come to pass; he shall have whatsoever he saith' (whatever you're saying) He said you are going to have whatever you say.

We were talking about travailing prayer. Lord how did I get off into that? I guess somebody needed it because somebody is considering divorce. No, I can't take it! I can't go through it! I can't make it! I can't do it Jesus. I can't!

There have been some people that went and got a divorce and God put them back together. There are some people they didn't have any business getting married to begin with. There are some people that God have put together that the devil has come and tried to destroy that relationship. They don't want to give God the credit for what God can do. But if God bless you with a spouse, men and women just don't know how beautiful it is when God put two people together.

COMMANDED TO FORGIVE

But you got some people that just don't know how to forgive. They've been hurt. They've been wronged. They've been abused. We're all human. We're subject to make mistakes sometimes, to do things and say things. But I realize and I don't care what happens or what goes on, we must be willing to forgive. I've known, I've been acquainted with grief, sorrow and pain just like the son of God him self. Isaiah testified of Christ, 'he was a man acquainted with grief and sorrow. We hid as it was our faces from him.' Jesus wasn't married. Jesus was the Son of God. (cf. Isa. 53:3)

There are some people that are being pressured into doing some things. You got to watch the peer pressure. You got people just don't want to see you happy, blessed. They will talk against your spouse. Keep those kinds of people out of your house. You have no business telling your mother or your family members what goes on between you and your husband. If there is no physical abuse involved, you just need to get with your spouse and pray. Sometimes verbal abuse is just as bad, were you give it word for word. Then you say things to hurt one another. I've been there. That's why I'm saying these things. I'm not ashamed. I know what I'm talking about. I got experience and can minister along those lines. Somebody needs this tonight. I don't mind taking a side journey. Lord you just do whatever you want to do. I'm yielding to your spirit.

I said I've been there! I know sorrow! I know hurt! I know when you love somebody and they tell you, 'I don't love you anymore!' It's over! That's it! I don't love you anymore!' I've had my heart broken. I shed many of tears. I pleaded with God—nothing happened. But God said son it's not over yet. God said I'm just making you a man of God. I want to emphasize this. I got to stop right here. The spirit of God is dealing with me…

MARRIAGE: BETWEEN A MAN AND A WOMAN

The Bible says 'Marriage is honorable in all, and the bed undefiled: but whoremongers and adulterers God will judge.' (Hebrews 13:4)

God put a man here on this earth in the garden. Adam was alone. God took a rib from Adam and made a woman. She shall be called a woman because she came from the womb of a man. God didn't call a woman to be behind a man. He didn't call her to be in front of him. He pulled her out of his side to be right by his side and a help meet. God said I shall make (not a help mate but a help meet) for him. But that's the same as saying a help mate.

Some people get married and in a couple of years their love wear out and wears off. After they've gone on the honeymoon the love just kind of subside a little bit. The love wanes. Why, because the same thing it took for you to get your spouse, it's going to take for you to keep them, the love of God.

But some of you say Brother Martin, I'm serving the Lord, walking with Jesus and my wife has backslidden and went back into the world. She's got another man. Oh Jesus... She doesn't want to come back to God. My husband doesn't want to come back to God. What am I supposed to do? You continuously walk with Jesus that's what you do. Set your face like a flint and walk with God. My heart aches and my heart hurts for people that let the devil use them to walk out on one another to destroy their life and their marriage. I've been there.

You people are here tonight that I'm talking about. I can call you out right now. I'm not talking about anything you told me. I can tell you something you said yourself. You didn't tell me anything. I can tell you what the Lord said. I had to come this way tonight because the people were not here the other night so I couldn't say it. But God said you say it tonight son. I'm not going to get back on Travailing prayer. I'm going to stay right here where God is telling me to because somebody needs this. The devil's been trying to break up some marriages, but I'm going to stop him. I'm going to stop the devil tonight. I'm going stop you tonight devil!

How many love God? How many know God loves you? How many know that God is on your side? The Bible says marriage is honorable in all and the bed undefiled. God ordained the family. He ordained marriage. There is no ordaining or appointing on of girlfriend or boyfriend relationships. When you say those vows, they mean something. Those vows are sacred. We take them lightly. Some people have gotten into some relationships, some marriage, and it has cost them something because they didn't consider.

Marriage is like a seed. It has to grow. The relationship has to be cultivated between two people. In the word of God, I read the letter of the Apostle Paul. He said I wish that all men were even as I. Paul said when you are married you got to care about the things of the world. But when you are not married you can be concerned about the things of the Lord. But the people that are married, they got to care about the things of this life. People that are not married, you can be busier for God. But when you find two married people committed and dedicated to God, you can be just the same way busy for God. Those are the words of Paul

Some things in the Bible, Paul said, I don't have anything of the Lord—this is just my own opinion. Those were some things that Paul said himself. Paul said I'm being honest. The Lord didn't say it, but I'm just saying it because I think it ought to be this way. But then Paul said I think I also have the spirit of God.

Well, I think I also have the spirit of God. Don't let my age fool you and deceive you—just as Paul told Timothy: when folks have a desire to look down on you, Paul said let no man despise thy youth. One thing I found out about the word of God, when you are sharp in the word of God, when you study and do your homework you can be like Jesus when he went in that temple before all those elders, the Pharisees and the Scribes. Jesus was sharp in the word! They couldn't catch him in anything.

That's why it is so important to study so that when people come to check you out and to be critical, you can give them the word of God. Let them know that you know that God has called you. You don't have to lift up yourself. People will know. Jesus said my sheep know my voice. One thing about it, if you are called of God, you're going to be humble. 'You're going to be wise as a serpent and harmless as a dove.' (Matt. 10:16) And you're not going to lift up yourself but you are going to lift up him self.

Why, because you have denied yourself. You have taken up your cross and you are following him. Jesus said 'if I be lifted up from the earth, I will draw all men nigh unto me.' (John 12:32) You're not going to lift up yourself, when you're called, anointed and appointed of God. You're going to lift up Jesus! You're going to give glory to God! Why, because Jesus didn't lift up himself. He lifted up the Father. God didn't lift up himself. He lifted up the Son. The Holy Spirit didn't lift up himself. He lifted up Jesus!

REFLECTION AND STUDY

1. Discuss natural childbirth and labor in comparison to spiritual birthing.

2. Romans 8:22 says for we now that the whole creation _____ and _____ in pain together until now.

3. When a person is in pain or they are suffering, they're going to _____ and _____. They travail in spirit and give birth to things.

4. Compare Revelation 12:2 to Isaiah 66:6-9.

5. Real travail concerns the _____ that we put into our praying.

6. Do we have to worry about what's going to take place in ministry or our lives?

7. Can we pray and get the victory in our spirit before a thing occurs?

8. What does 1st John 4:4 say about overcoming?

9. Describe attributes of the Spirit that will help you travail in prayer?

10. The Apostle Paul said to the Galatians Church in 4:19 my little children of whom I _____ in birth again until _____ be formed in you.

11. Prayer is fellowshipping and _____ forces with God. Teaching is _____ and Preaching is proclaiming.

12. In 1st Corinthians 13 the Apostle Paul discuses _____.

13. Paul said when he was a _____ he spoke as a child but when he became a man he put away childish things.

14. Do some Christians act like children, not coming to the point were they allow the word of God to rule and govern their lives? Discuss the dying process as your inward man is renewed day by day.

15. There is a great falling away in the body. Some people rather put their eyes on a leader rather than God and when the leader falls their god has fallen. How should you be consecrated and dedicated to God to guard against this?

16. If a house is divided you may have to walk alone. (True or False)

17. What does Eph. 4:32 say about love and forgiveness?

18. What does Eph. 5 say about husbands and wives loving one another? Discuss submission to one another?

19. When there's a problem sometimes we talk too much and look at what the devil is doing rather than _____. You got to be careful what you say in your homes and in your relationships. Proverbs 18:21 says what about the tongue?

20. We are all human and some things we've gone through in life cause pain, hurt and sorrow. In Isaiah 53:5 Jesus was also a man acquainted with grief, despised and rejected. How can his example help you to handle life's challenges?

21. Discuss peer pressure from your family, friends and associates concerning your marriage or other significant relationships.

22. In Hebrews 13:4 what does God say about marriage?

23. Will the devil break up a marriage if you let him? If a person walks out on you, you should set you face like a _____ and continue to walk with Jesus.

24. Marriage is like a seed, it has to _____. It has to be cultivated by both people. Lift up the Father, the Son and the Holy Spirit in your relationships.

PART II

The POWER AND FIRE!
OF JESUS CHURCH

"There is nothing that God won't do in you, through you and for you if you have faith in him and believe him."

4.2

The Apostle Paul said in 2nd Corinthians 5:17 'if any man be in Christ' (I'm in Christ and he is on the inside of me). You are in Christ and he is on the inside of you. Paul said 'if any man be in Christ, he is a new creature' (or creation) 'behold all things are passed away and all things become new.'

When you get through dying daily, you can die to those attitudes. You can die to that temper you got. You can die to that bitterness. You can die to that malice. You can die to un-forgiveness because when you get through fasting and praying, you're not going to want to be bitter. If you're having a problem in your marriage, and you start fasting and praying you're going to want to love your spouse. But you got to die!

Paul said in 1st Corinthians 9:27 'but I keep under my body and bring it into subjection: lest that by any means, when I have preached to others, I myself should be a castaway.' He said I bring this flesh up under subjection. Some of you folks that are having problems with the flesh—die daily! Mortify your members therefore. Crucify the flesh. Walk in the spirit. What is the spirit? The word is the spirit. Walk in the word and you will not fulfill the lust and the desires of the flesh!

I want you to know that you are more than a conqueror. God said neigh in all these things you're more than a conqueror. Paul said who or what shall separate us from the love of God? Neither death, nor life, nor angels, nor principalities, nor powers, nor things present, nor things to come. I am persuaded Paul said, nothing shall separate us from the love of Christ—shall tribulation, distress, persecution, famine, nakedness, peril or sword—nothing! Paul was fully persuaded. Paul said I've committed everything unto him. I've given everything to him. I've committed my all to him. That was a revelation when Paul talked about being conformable to Christ death. (cf. Romans 8)

When you're conformable to Christ death, it is no more you! When you stand up and minster, it is not you, it is Jesus! When you lay hands on the sick, you're going to see Jesus healing the sick. That's what I do. When I speak to people that are in wheel chairs, I see them walking—calling things that be not as though they already were.
(cf. Romans 4:17)

Psalms 33:9 says 'God spoke and it was done. Let it be! He commanded and it stood fast.' God is trying to bring us into a place of faith. Yes! I'm tying to bring you into a place of faith. Without faith it is impossible to please God! 'For, he that cometh to God must believe that he is.' (Hebrew 11:6)

Enoch had this testimony that he pleased God. His testimony was a testimony of faith. You look in Hebrews the 11th chapter, it says by faith Abel..., by faith Noah..., by faith Abraham..., by faith Moses..., by faith Joseph..., through faith Sarah received strength (faith is a strength) She received strength to have a baby at the age of ninety. There is nothing that God won't do in you, through you and for you if you have faith in him and believe him. I'm talking about according to the word of God: The 1stEpistle of John 5:14 says 'And this is the confidence that we have in him, that, if we ask any thing according to his will' God's word is his will. Listen! We got the promise of God. God's given you a promise. We are in covenant with God. God's got to fulfill his covenant. The word of God says:

'That by two immutable things, in which it was impossible for God to lie' (Hebrews 6:18)

'God is not a man that he should lie' (Numbers 23:19)

'Let God be true, but every man a liar' (Romans 3:4)

God's word is true! People say man you are well versed. I study my Bible and that's why I'm well versed. And I'm not walking in the flesh. I'm walking in the spirit. Jesus said in Matthew 5:6:

'Blessed are they which do hunger and thirst after righteousness: for they shall be filled!'
John 7:38 'He that believeth on me, as the scripture hath said, out of his belly shall flow rivers of living water!'

Psalms 119:130 'The entrance of thy words giveth light; it giveth understanding unto the simple!'

Psalms 119:105 'Thy word is a lamp unto my feet, and a light unto my path!'

David said in Psalms 119:11 'Thy word have I hid in mine heart, that I might not sin against thee.'

He said you will have this seed that will remain in you. You cannot sin. He didn't say you would not sin but you cannot sin. Why, because that seed is Christ. First Peter talks about the incorruptible seed. That's why you have to be born again. You have been born of a natural birth but you have to be born again. Elder Peterson said rebirth. Do you know what gets born again when you get born again? Your spirit gets born again. You are a new man. That's why Paul said 'if any man be born again he is a new creature' (cf. 2 Corinthians 5:17)

That's why Jesus told Nicodemus, that religious ruler, you must be born again. Nicodemus said how can I go back into my mother's womb and be born again? Nicodemus was a very intelligent and intellectual man. He knew the law. He was well versed in the law but he didn't know the simplicity of what it was to be born again. That's why he came to Jesus by night. Nicodemus was notable—a big man. He came to Jesus by night. He said unto him 'Rabbi, we know that thou art a teacher come from God: for no man can do these miracles that thou doest, except God be with him.' God was not only with Jesus, he was in Jesus doing the miracles. (cf. John 3)

120

SENSITIVE TO THE SPIRIT OF GOD

We've been talking about Travailing prayer. For the last past two nights we talked about Prevailing prayer—how Jacob prevailed with God. The angel said let me go. Jacob said I will not let thee go except thy bless me. That's like a child of God down there saying, God I'm not going to get up off of my knees until God you give me the victory! Like that woman in Luke's gospel chapter 18:1 'Jesus spoke a parable unto this end that men ought always to pay and not to faint.'

You find folks instead of 'ought to pray' they ought to argue. They ought to get into griping. They ought to get into complaining. They ought to get into fussing when they ought to be praying. That's why people are fainthearted. They come to me on my doorstep crying. They come to me calling all times of night. I can't even get into prayer. A lot of times, I sacrifice for people when I should be praying. I can't just do people any kind of way. I got the love off God in me. You can't just push people off and throw them off. It might be important. Somebody's life might be at stake. And you're insensitive to the spirit of God saying, 'I got to go pray!' 'Call me back later.' You're some kind of minister. You must be a devilish minister. You don't have the love of Christ.

Not one person that came to Jesus did he push them off. I find Jesus during the day time in ministry but at night I find him in all night prayer to God. When you are in all night prayer with God and you come out, miracles are going to take place. Devils will be cast out and sick bodies will be healed.

I just tell people, I'm a Jesus preacher. I believe it all. I believe in casting out devils, healing the sick and raising the dead. Everything Jesus said, I believe in doing it. Jesus said in John 14:12 'Verily, verily, I say unto you, he that believeth on me, the works that I do shall he do also: and greater works than these shall he do; because I go unto my Father.'

How many here believe on Jesus? Well we ought to be doing the works that he did. When Jesus sent his disciples out, he gave them power over the devil. Sickness is a devil! Aid's is a devil! Jesus gave them power over unclean spirits. He gave them power to heal all sickness and disease. He gave them power to raise the dead. He gave them power to cleanse the lepers! What's wrong with the church? Where is the power church? Where is the power?

Jesus said in Matthew 16:18 'And I say also unto thee, that thou art Peter, and upon this rock I will build my church; and the gates of hell shall not prevail against it!' Jesus Church is not some little weak minimized church that's backed up from the devil. Jesus church is a church baptized in the power and the fire of Almighty God that's standing in faith and they declare the word of God:

Daniel 11:32 says 'those that know their God shall be strong and do exploits!'

God said in Luke 10:9 'Behold, I give unto you power to tread on serpents and scorpions, and over all the power of the enemy: and nothing shall by any means hurt you. God's given you power over the devil!'

Jesus said in Matthew 18:18 'whatsoever you bind on earth, shall be bound in heaven and whatsoever you loose on earth shall be loosed in heaven!'

You got authority to bind the devil up! If he's in your home, bind him up! He's in your marriage bind him up! He's got a hold to your money, loose your money in Jesus name! Bind the devil up because *greater is he that is in thee that he that is in the world.* The word of God says in Romans 8:31 'if God be for us who can be against us?' God's on your side! David said if it had not been for the Lord on our side where would I be. I read in Isaiah 54:17 'No weapon that is formed against thee shall prosper: and every tongue that shall rise against thee in judgment thou shall condemn!'

Jesus said 'it's my meat to do the will of him that sent me.' He said 'labor not for that meat which perisheth but labor unto that which endureth unto eternal life.' Jesus said in the word of God 'I am the very resurrection! I am the life!' He said 'I am the way, the truth and the life!' Jesus said 'I've come that you might have life and have it more abundantly!' God has come to bring you the abundant life. You are not defeated! (cf. John 6:27, 11:5, 14:16, and 10:10)

The 1st Epistle of John 5:4 says 'for whatsoever is born of God overcometh the world: and this is the victory that overcometh the world, even our faith!'

The word of God says in 2nd Corinthians 5:7 'for we walk by faith, not by sight.'
Hebrews 11:1 says 'now faith is' (not was! Not is going to be) Faith is! 'The substance of things hoped for, the evidence of things not seen.'

The Bible says Abraham faith was counted for righteousness. He was called a friend of God. Abraham's faith brought him to a right relationship with God. God didn't look on him as a sinner. He looked on him as a righteous man as a saved man. Why, because he believed the word of God. Abraham took God—at his word! The word of God says:

'Call unto me, and I will answer thee, and show thee great and might things, which thou knowest not.' (Jeremiah 33:3)

God said in Jeremiah 32:27 'Behold, I am the LORD, the God of all flesh: is there anything too hard for me?'

APOSTOLIC AUTHORITY

God is moving on your behalf. It may seem impossible. Jesus said 'the things that are impossible with men are possible with God if you only believe oh ye of little faith.' Some of you have weak faith but you ought to declare that you are strong in faith. You ought to say I'm full of faith. Let it be your confession. You might not be there right now but if you keep saying it long enough you're going to be full. You are going to have what you say! I say I'm full of faith! I say I'm strong in faith! I say I'm full of faith and power! I'm full of faith and power!

Devil you better get out of my way because I'm going to tread upon you! Jesus said in the word of God that he has given you power to tread (that means to walk on scorpions and serpents) every demon spirit you can walk over. God's given you power! God's given you authority over the devil. He's given you power over sickness and disease. He said ye shall lay your hands (a believer) on the sick and they shall recover!

God spoke to me sitting in the car tonight. He said, son you are going to walk in full Apostolic authority tonight. He said that Apostle ministry—all that stuff is going to come out. I said God you do what you want to do. Thank you Lord. I'm just letting the river flow. Go ahead Holy Ghost. Have your way and bless your people!

The Bible says in Isaiah 65:24 'and it shall come to pass, that before they call. I will answer: and while they are yet speaking, I will hear.' I want you to know God done already heard and answered your prayer before you even prayed it. He knows what you're thinking before you even thought it. God knows the very desires of your heart. But he said if you delight yourself in the Lord then he shall give you the desires of your heart. How do you delight yourself in the Lord? You delight yourself in the Law of the Lord. God told Joshua:

> 'This book of the law shall not depart out of thy mouth; but thou shalt meditate therein day and night, that thou mayest observe to do according to all that is written therein: for then thou shalt make thy way prosperous, and then thou shalt have good success.! The amplified says thou shall deal wisely in all the affairs of life.' (Joshua 1:8)

We need to turn our plate down and get on our face before God and let God pour into us. Proverbs 4:7 says 'wisdom is the principle thing.' We need the wisdom of God. God gave it to Solomon. Solomon didn't ask God for wealth. He didn't ask God for honor and riches. Do you know what comes with wisdom? Wealth, honor, riches and long life comes with wisdom.

However, Solomon backslid because he messed around with strange women. When God tell you not to do something and tell you to leave that thing alone, leave it alone because it will get you into trouble. It will be the very thing to destroy you. God begins to use us and bless us, and then we get lifted up. People begin to worship us and see us as gods. That's when God got to allow us to be made low. We get into sin and we mess up. When people begin to worship you and they get their eyes on you, God is not going to like it. God said he will not give his praise, or his glory, or his honor to flesh. So we must lift up Jesus. We must lift up the spirit of God. We must lift up Christ!

TRANSPARENT MINISTRY

I feel the anointing in my hands. As I sat in the car tonight God said, son I'm going to use your hands tonight. I said, Lord you do whatever you want to do. I haven't prayed for people in three nights. I haven't laid hands on anybody because I haven't been directed by God to do so. I don't play church. I don't play with God. I don't play with the anointing. I don't play with the Holy Ghost. I don't play with the ministry because I'm standing in a spot that if I know my life is not right, I will die here.

That's what's going to happen when preachers don't clean their lives up. They're going to die. If they don't come forth and confess their mess, they are going to die. You better believe that's what God told me and that's why I'm getting my life straight. That's why I'm getting my act together because I don't want to be one of them that stand behind here and fool you. Yet all the while God knows that I got junk in my own life. I can fool you but I can't fool God. I'm talking about myself now. I'm not ashamed to say it. That's why I need your prayers. You might think or say Apostle Martin you got it all together. No I don't I'm human just like you. I got this word and I love this word and I believe in not just being a hearer and a reader but I believe in being a doer of the word.

God blesses a doer, not just a reader and a hearer, but a doer of the word. James said don't be merely listeners or hearers but be ye doers of the word. God blesses a doer of the word of God. Some of you in here are going to sleep. You come to church to sleep. Wake up! Wake up! I don't like folks sleeping in my meetings. I'm going to throw the Bible at some of you. (*He jokingly says*) I'm going to throw it and hit you with the word. Somebody will ask: What did you do Brother Martin to that young man? I hit him with the word. This is the word isn't it?

That's a true story though. One brother really told that testimony in church. A brother and his wife were having some problems and he hit her with the word. She went and told the pastor. The pastor asked her, what's that little mark right there? She said, pastor, he hit me with the word. He shouldn't have hit her like that though. Sometimes when a preacher is preaching we get hit with the word. I'm through tonight. We are going to minister to some of you:

PRAYER FOR THE WOMAN

How many of you love the Lord? Is there anybody here tonight that's been having pain in your lower back? Is that you Ms, Sir? Come up here and we're going to minister to you. In the lower back that's where the pain is. Come here my sister and lay your right hand on her lower back. Ms lift up your hands and close your eyes and Jesus is going to touch you right now: Father, in Jesus name, God as I lay my hands upon my dear precious sister, Father I bind and rebuke the pain in her back in Jesus name! I command the pain to go from her back now! There it is. Gods anointing is going into your back right now. There it is. Receive it. Let Him bless you. God's touching you right now. Give God the praise!

PRAYER FOR A MAN

Father, in the name of the Lord Jesus Christ, as I lay my hands upon this dear precious Elder, God I ask you to touch him right now from the crown of his head to the soles of his feet. I bind and rebuke the back pain and I command it to go right now in Jesus name. Devil you're trespassing on private property. Satan! In Jesus name, take your hands off of him. Now! There it is sir. The power of God is going into your back right now. Give God the praise and thank him.

PRAYER FOR A BROTHER

Brother God's going to bless you financially. Hold your hands up and claim it. Father, in Jesus name, I thank you for doing it for him God. I thank you for meeting that financial need. God's doing it for him. Prosperity!

TESTIMONY OF A BABY HEALED

This sister right here! You got a testimony. Is that the same baby that we prayed for? Sister I've been asking God to let you come back and testify. In a three night meeting that we had, God blessed us and gave that baby a miracle. That baby had a heart condition and was scheduled to have surgery but God healed that baby. When she went back to the doctor's the doctor's didn't understand it but that baby was healed, and I want that testimony. By the blood of the lamb and the words of our testimony we overcome. The Bible says in *Revelation 12:11 and they overcame him by the blood of the Lamb and by the word of their testimony; and they loved not their lives unto the death.*

1. 2nd Cor. 5:17 says: 'If any man be in _____ he is a ____ creature'.

2. When you get born again the old things you used to do that did not glorify God should pass away. (True or False)

3. This is a part of the dying process: dying to your attitude, temper, malice, un-forgiveness, bitterness and hatred. (True or False)

4. What example does 1st Cor. 9:27 gives us to do what with our bodies—our flesh?

5. If you walk in the word and walk in the _____ you won't fulfill the lust of the _____.

6. According to Romans 8:38 who and what can separate us from the love of God?

7. Romans 4:17 instructs us to _____ things that be not as though they were.

8. God is trying to bring us to a place of faith. Heb. 11:6 says without _____ it is _____ to please God.

9. Discuss some of those who demonstrated faith that Paul talks about in Hebrews 11.

10. What does 1st John 5:14 say about faith and confidence?

11. What does Hebrews 6:18 say about Gods word?

12. Jesus said in John 7:38 he that _____ on me, as the _____ says out of his _____ shall flow rivers of living water.

13. When you get born again, it is your spirit that gets born again. (True or False)

14. In John 3 even though Nicodemous was well versed in the law, what was it that he did not understand?

15. Nicodemus came to Jesus by night. Some of us came to Jesus by night and when we are in different places in the world such as on the job, at a friends, etc. we don't want anyone to know. (True or False)

16. Jesus said pray always. Instead of praying always some people are always arguing, complaining, griping and grumbling. (True or False)

17. Because of a lack of prayer people end up faint-hearted and needing to be ministered to. (True or False)

18. Not one person who came to Jesus did he push off. In the day you find Jesus _____ at night you find him in _____ with God.

20. When Jesus spoke to Peter in Matthew 16:18 about a spirit of prevail was he talking to the church today too?

21. What does Daniel 11:32 say about strength?

22. Discuss power according to Luke 10:9.

23. Matthew 18:18 says what about binding and loosing?

24. What does Isaiah 54:17 say about adversaries and their weapons?

25. 2nd Cor. 5:7 says that we walk by _____ and not by _____.

26. Abraham, called the Father of faith, took God at his _____.

27. In Jer. 32:27 God said call unto me and I will show you what?

28. If you are weak in faith you need to keep _____ that you are strong. For you will eventually have what you _____.

29. In Luke 10:19 Jesus gave us power to _____ upon the enemy.

30. Discuss walking in full Apostolic power.

31. What shall come to pass according to Isaiah 65:24?

32. God said delight yourself in me and I will give you the desires of your heart. (True or False)

33. In Joshua 8 what did God say about His word?

34. We need to turn our _____ down and get on our _____ before God and let God pour into us.

35. We need wisdom. What does Proverbs 4:7 say about wisdom? What comes with wisdom?

36. When God lifts us up we must be careful not to take his glory. A minister can perhaps stand before people and fool them if their life is not straight but they can't fool God. (True or False)

37. You got to not only be a _____ and a hearer but a _____ of God's word.

EPILOGUE

Indeed we are over-comers by the blood of the Lamb and the testimony of what Jesus has done for us. The testimony of Jesus is the spirit of prophecy. (Rev. 19:10) This book is about the word of that testimony. The fourth cassette captures the conclusion of the services. Yet, the tapes did not capture the full service. The woman did come forth and give the testimony. That baby was healed and hasn't had a heart problem since. Today he is twenty years old, in college and lives in Fort Lauderdale.

In Section I, Prevailing prayer, on page sixty of this book is a story similar to Mary Magdalene of whom Jesus cast out seven devils. Apostle Martin also cast devils out of that young lady. Later, one night, for an unknown reason, other than just enjoying making people happy and giving gifts this same young lady brought a set of crystal praying hands to church to give to Pastor Bullard and his wife. Apostle Martin saw her with the set of crystal praying hands. At the next service he brought the Four-part tape series on prayer and gave it to her. He also gave her a single tape that he preached called Power to Cast out Demons & Devils. Unfortunately, this tape was loaned out and never received back.

I am that young lady that he gave the tape series too. Well not as young anymore but still young at heart, love the Lord, his people and souls; who certainly came to believe and honor what Jesus commanded: Men ought always pray and not faint.

After he gave me the tapes, every now and then I would listen to them briefly. After three months I listened to them fully and when I heard the second tape, I said "Oh!" "That's me!" Prior to this happening, I had no inner knowledge that he cast devils out of me. I just knew I was changed. Over the course of twenty years the Four-tape series on prayer survived. From time to time over the twenty years I have played them. The word always seemed so fresh as if spoken yesterday. They never wore out. I believe Apostle is smiling over the banisters of heaven just as I saw him in a dream in 2008. He said to me, "I gave you Prevailing, Travailing and Intercessory Prayer." It was in greater Atlanta, Stone Mountain, GA where I felt impressed of the Lord to transcribe these tapes and put into a book format. I began the process 2007 and stopped but in September 2008 a messenger from Satan continually came to buffet me, being in the midst of tremendous warfare, I began transcribing again.

My mentors, those teachings on the tapes along with prayer and worship helped me to walk out what I was going through and watch as the hand of God performed a miracle and brought me out. So I encourage you as you read this book, pray always and walk out your faith. For God is good! God is great! And 'he daily loadeth us with benefits.' (Ps. 68) Prevailing prayer don't talk defeat. Travailing prayer not only brings to birth, but delivers and Intercessory prayer takes on the cause and pleads the case before the throne room of God until they get the victory. Yes, this book is about prayer and deliverance too. I see Apostle Martin now as he stands—before, we the people continuing to teach:

> "There is no problem to big that God can't solve it. There is no mountain to tall that God can't move it. There is no sorrow to deep that he can't soothe it. There's no storm to dark that God can't calm it!"

And again I say: "IT'S FINISHED!"
Prophetess Debbie Jerido

134

OTHER RESOURCES

RIVERS OF WATERS
PRO CHOICE

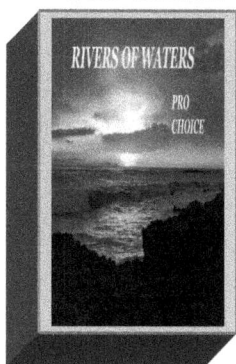

Powerful & Anointed! Appointed for such a time as this! Ever experience tremendous pain in life? Your eyes ever felt like a reservoir of tears? This memoir explores some of life's deepest questions: Like why does evil exist? Why do bad things happen to good people? Identify stressors within and without and learn to **avoid spiritual abortion**. Deal effectively with the politically correct, controversial issues of this age. Enter the mysteries of the dream world and confront the stakes for your soul. Boldly go where man dares not to go, where the secrets of the heart lye.

STRONG WINDS
Strong Women Win!

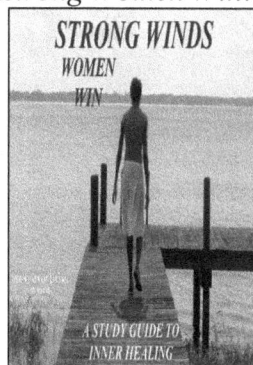

NO ISSUE TO DEEP that God can't heal it! *An eight-week plan* and Heart to Heart Interactive, practical Study guide to Inner Healing. Concepts can be utilized by both men and women. For group study or by individuals. Space for journal entries. Experience a Mega-Shift in your life.

An optional set of companion **Abundant Life Skills** 'Free' with purchase of Strong Winds. Used in conjunction with the book to assist with practical life management such as Employment, Housing, Parenting Skills, Relationship management, etc.

(Free) Bible Study Guides are self-paced and can be obtained by request. When one is complete another guide can be requested. Separate studies available on the four gospels Matthew, Mark, Luke and John. It is recommended that you start with the Book of Saint Mark.

FOUNDATION FOR SUCCESS

BY APOSTLE CALVIN MARTIN

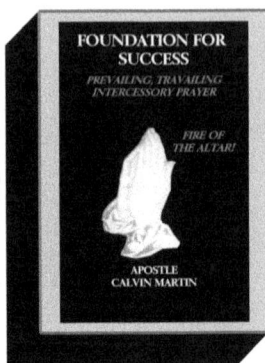

(Hardcover edition)   available
(Soft cover edition)   available

PREVAILING, TRAVAILING, INTERCESSORY PRAYER. Birthing the Christos, apostolic, anointing to cast out demons and devils, heal the sick, heal the wounded and the broken-hearted. Where power with God gets you power with man as you walk into your destiny and fulfill the ministry call to intercessory prayer. God has a voice and he speaks by it. Learn to distinguish the voice of God who is a Person.

Order online

For books, Abundant Life Skills, CD's, tapes, DVD's, Bible Study

Guides and related materials. We'd also like to pray with you and

believe God for your miracle so send your prayer request via email at

www.FndForLivingwater.com

Or email us at FNDForLivingwater@gmail.com

www.ingramcontent.com/pod-product-compliance
Lightning Source LLC
Chambersburg PA
CBHW061951070426
42450CB00007BA/1194